THE SCROLL OF YESHAYAHU

The Unfolding Reflections
of the Ancient and
Coming Worlds — Judah, Jerusalem,
and the Ends of the Earth

Xavier Montañez

WESTBOW
PRESS®
A DIVISION OF THOMAS NELSON
& ZONDERVAN

Copyright © 2020 Xavier Montañez.

All rights reserved. No part of this book may be used or reproduced by any means, graphic, electronic, or mechanical, including photocopying, recording, taping or by any information storage retrieval system without the written permission of the author except in the case of brief quotations embodied in critical articles and reviews.

This book is a work of non-fiction. Unless otherwise noted, the author and the publisher make no explicit guarantees as to the accuracy of the information contained in this book and in some cases, names of people and places have been altered to protect their privacy.

WestBow Press books may be ordered through booksellers or by contacting:

WestBow Press
A Division of Thomas Nelson & Zondervan
1663 Liberty Drive
Bloomington, IN 47403
www.westbowpress.com
844-714-3454

Because of the dynamic nature of the Internet, any web addresses or links contained in this book may have changed since publication and may no longer be valid. The views expressed in this work are solely those of the author and do not necessarily reflect the views of the publisher, and the publisher hereby disclaims any responsibility for them.

Any people depicted in stock imagery provided by Getty Images are models, and such images are being used for illustrative purposes only.
Certain stock imagery © Getty Images.

ISBN: 978-1-6642-0192-7 (sc)
ISBN: 978-1-6642-0194-1 (hc)
ISBN: 978-1-6642-0193-4 (e)

Library of Congress Control Number: 2020914947

Print information available on the last page.

WestBow Press rev. date: 08/26/2020

Unless otherwise indicated, all Scripture taken from the New King James Version®. Copyright © 1982 by Thomas Nelson. Used by permission. All rights reserved.

Scripture quotations taken from the New American Standard Bible® (NASB), Copyright © 1960, 1962, 1963, 1968, 1971, 1972, 1973, 1975, 1977, 1995 by The Lockman Foundation Used by permission. www.Lockman.org

Scripture marked (WEB) taken from the World English Bible.

Scripture quotations marked (ESV) are from the ESV® Bible (The Holy Bible, English Standard Version®), copyright © 2001 by Crossway, a publishing ministry of Good News Publishers. Used by permission. All rights reserved.

Scripture quotations marked (NIV) are taken from the Holy Bible, New International Version®, NIV®. Copyright © 1973, 1978, 1984, 2011 by Biblica, Inc.™ Used by permission of Zondervan. All rights reserved worldwide. www.zondervan.com The "NIV" and "New International Version" are trademarks registered in the United States Patent and Trademark Office by Biblica, Inc.™

Scripture marked (OJB) taken from The Orthodox Jewish Bible Copyright 20 by AFI International. All rights reserved.

Scripture marked (KJV) taken from the King James Version of the Bible.

To my father,
who first allowed me to ask questions.

CONTENTS

Preface xiii
Introduction xv

PART 1: HOMOLOGOUSLY ENCRYPTED
1. A Mile-High Synopsis 1
2. Structural Similarities 8
3. Old Testament Parallels 17
4. New Testament Parallels 22

PART 2: PANORAMIC PERSPECTIVES
5. Bucket A: Historical Predictions (800 BC–1 BC) 39
6. Identifying the Lord's Servant 58
7. Bucket B: Messianic Predictions 65
8. Bucket C: Eschatological Predictions 73

PART 3: VISIONS OF DIVINE PERSONALITY
9. Logical Blunders 89
10. Eschatological Mix-Ups 94
11. New Testament Allusions 102

APPENDIX
A Question of Authorship: Did More Than One
Person Write Isaiah? 114

References 123

TABLE OF FIGURES

0.1	Book of Isaiah, Dead Sea Scrolls	xvii
2.1	Old Testament Organization Schemes	10
4.1	Overview of Homologous Structures	36
5.1	Isaiah's Prophetic Timeline and Designation of Buckets	40
5.2	Isaiah's Prophetic Timeline and Designation of Buckets	41
5.3	Assyrian Invasion of Israeli-Syrian Alliance	42
5.4	Assyria's failed invasion of Judah	44
5.5	Babylonian Invasion of Assyria	46
5.6	Egyptian cities with Jewish Quarters	54
6.1	Uses of the word "Servant" from Ch. 40–53	58
6.2	References to Jacob and Israel from Ch. 40–53	63
8.1	Summarizing Isaiah's Prophecies	85
9.1	The Root and the Shoot of Jesse	91
11.1	Summary of Divine Attributes and Personalities in Isaiah	112
A.1	Similar Uses of Language in Both Halves of Isaiah	118

PREFACE

The impetus for the present work is, with all sincerity, to be found at the feet of Mr. David Pawson, British international Bible expositor.

It was during one of his seminars in May of 2011, while I attended the Forerunner School of Ministry in Kansas City, Missouri, that the seeds that later became this volume were planted.

During the course of his lecture entitled "How to Study the Bible," many of my previously held perspectives on the scriptures were absolutely shattered—perspectives which were formed over the course of twenty years of one who had grown up in the church, a convinced believer in Jesus and avid reader of the Bible.

For decades I had read and even memorized scriptures devoid of their true context. Personally, I was convicted of this practice and felt the need to rectify the situation.

I proposed to reread all the scriptures starting from Genesis, however, my zeal was quickly exhausted somewhere between Leviticus and Numbers. Perhaps my goal was too ambitious, so instead, I simplified the task, aiming to fully comprehend just one single book.

And so in the summer of 2011 I began to study the prophet Isaiah, only to be surprised by the richness and depth of his writings. Initially, I had no intentions of producing any sort of written volume; my main objective was simply to study the scriptures and rectify this decades-long disinformation and biblical deficiency. However, along the journey of attempting to understand this one book, oftentimes I was asked questions about faith and scripture, for which, surprisingly, it seemed that material from Isaiah could provide an adequate answer.

When certain questions (or problems) arose more than once, I decided proper documentation was needed, particularly because of my terrible memory, thus enabling me to reference the content more efficiently. The answers to such questions are in essence what this work is composed of. These were questions that cover topics on faith and reason; questions like "Do we have adequate grounds for believing the scriptures to be true?"; questions on hermeneutics, Bible study, and the deity of Jesus.

Thus, my hope is not only that this work will serve as a launching pad into the study of the scriptures, much as Mr. Pawson's lecture did for me, but also as we examine the contents of the prophet Isaiah, building on a foundation of the certainty of the Holy Scriptures, that they would come alive personally and you would be filled with a greater passion for the written word and ultimately the word made flesh, even Jesus Christ.

Xavier Montañez
Colorado Springs, Colorado
Spring 2020

INTRODUCTION

Penned in just forty years, the writings of Yeshayahu in the Great Isaiah Scroll entertain the subject matter of the past, present, and future with a divine and panoramic perspective.

Should the Egyptian pyramids or the edifices of Stonehenge be of human interest, the writings of Isaiah outshine them as more than a quaint reminder of bewildering achievements in civilizations past—indeed; a living document of the human story traced through the Hebraic nation.

Preserved in the caves of Qumran, the Great Isaiah Scroll is perhaps one of the most well-documented and complete ancient writings we have in our possession.[1] Today it lives in the collection of the Jewish and Christian Scriptures and is a remarkable document on many accounts.

In it we are presented with a myriad of astounding predictions: historical events spanning over a thousand years, specifics on the character of Israel's messiah, and accounts of the end of human history.

Yet, despite Isaiah's popularity among many, in modern times his writings have been largely misunderstood, neglected, and increasingly decontextualized; consequently, the richness of his prophecies has been lost.

In this compilation of reflections we will examine some of the most significant patterns, predictions, and theological messages in the document.

In Part 1, *Homologously Encrypted*, we examine the structure of Isaiah's document, making the startling discovery that the document as a whole appears to foreshadow the collection it is a part of—the canon of scriptures. We will get a grasp for the flow of the book in juxtaposition to the biblical scriptures in the Jewish Tanakh and New Testament writings.

In Part 2, *Panoramic Perspectives,* we will examine much of the text's predictive contents, tracing their fulfillment through historical documents or, where yet unfulfilled, expand on these futuristic predictions with the aid of complementary eschatological texts. In chapter 6, *Identifying the Lord's Servant,* we also explore the Servant Songs in Isaiah, a collection of four poems found in chapters 40–55.

Finally, in Part 3, *Visions of Divine Personality,* we will lay a defense for the deity of Messiah. No other prophet establishes the oneness of the creator as does Isaiah,[2] yet albeit somewhat paradoxically, numerous characters and personalities presented in the text appear to possess his divine attributes and responsibilities.

Each section includes a series of supplemental charts and visualizations to help summarize the content matter therein presented.

In the process, the reader will not only gain a deeper understanding of the book of Isaiah but will become better acquainted with the books of the Bible as a whole. These are great exercises for gaining familiarity with the scriptures and can be applied to the study of other biblical texts.

Finally, in the Appendix, we have also included considerations for questions on the authenticity and authorship of the text. Is Isaiah the work of a single author?

The study of Isaiah has inspired many throughout the ages, from *Messiah,* Handel's epic oratorio, to inscriptions on monuments at the United Nations headquarters.

I invite you on this journey in discovering the remarkable writings of Isaiah, I trust it will be nothing short of transformative.

Fig. 0.1: Book of Isaiah, Dead Sea Scrolls. In 1948 an entire copy of the book was unearthed in the caves of Qumran. Using carbon-14 dating methods, the age of the scrolls have been estimated to 335–324 BC.³ The copy of the original scroll is now housed at the Shrine of the Book in the Israel Museum (Jerusalem) and The Digital Dead Sea Scrolls can be viewed online in its entirety.⁴

PART 1

HOMOLOGOUSLY ENCRYPTED

A MILE-HIGH SYNOPSIS

CHAPTER ONE

> Time travel used to be thought of as just science fiction, but Einstein's general theory of relativity allows for the possibility that we could warp space-time so much that you could go off in a rocket and return before you set out.[1]
>
> —Stephen Hawking

Time. The fourth dimension of the physical realm has always been a topic of much intrigue to me. It is a constant reminder of the inconvenient truth that humans are but mortals, trapped in an ever-diminishing spatial continuum with no recourse of escape. Also fascinating, although time is such a ubiquitous concept to our everyday existences, providing an adequate definition of what exactly *time* is (at a more epistemic level) remains a daunting task. Attempts are usually self-referencing: one resorts to temporal (time-dependent) language and describes how time is measured as opposed to its actual *essence*.

In theory, scientists have long proposed that aberrations in space-time are possible;[2] in practice, however, we expect the physical realm to cohere with our standard notion of time; our daily existence depends on it.

This aberrant notion of natural time is what has made reading Isaiah's volume most captivating. His text, though clearly intended for a contemporary mid–eighth century audience, is many times written from the perspective of one existing outside this era—transcending the past, present, and future. It is written from the perspective of one who is not bound by time.

While I was previously aware of claims of foretelling in Isaiah (or even other prophetic literature in general for that matter), I was unaware of a certain interesting anomaly, one that appears to be an accident, further exemplifying this notion of timelessness. This chapter seeks to investigate that "accidental anomaly."

So here's the grand claim: upon examining the structure, organization, and subject matter presented in the ancient Isaiah scroll, we realize that it also mirrors the structure, organization, and subject matter of another very well-known compilation—one that would not be complete for another thousand years. We are referring here to none other than the books of the Bible in the Old and New Testaments—the canon of scriptures.

This foreshadowing of the complete standardized collection of biblical books centuries before its completion seemed to be another category of forecasting; one that was more difficult to fabricate, particularly when considering the archeological evidence supporting the authenticity and fidelity in transmission of this document.[3] It's as if the concept of the canon had been homologously encrypted in Isaiah's volume and transmitted unknowingly for centuries.

So let's dive right in. We will start by providing a brief overview of the content in Isaiah's volume and then proceed to compare its similarities in juxtaposition to the books of the Bible. We begin with a broad general purview, gradually becoming increasingly granular in our focus.

Studying Isaiah is a somewhat intimidating task not only because of its sheer volume but also because it is not very well organized. It isn't a topical or thematic composition flowing logically from one idea to the next as we are accustomed to in our standards of well-written publications. Rather, in Isaiah we have mostly a random compilation of writings from one man's forty-year-long career as a political adviser in the mid-eighth century.

Although Isaiah's work (which contains a collection of varying types of writings) is not organized in a typical fashion, it does have a shape and structure that helps in drawing the main themes and messages from his work. Below I have divided the book into sections where it seems the text has natural breaks and have provided a brief synopsis of the content therein. Take into consideration that most modern copies of the Bible contain chapters and verse numbers—divisions that were not part of the original text.[4] This formatting many times conceals the natural flow and genre of scripture. I believe this adds an unnecessary layer of difficulty in comprehension and interpretation. Fortunately, there are several translations available today that present these sacred writings in a much more readable and organic format. As we explore the contents of the Great Isaiah Scroll, the reader is encouraged to consult any such translations (e.g., WEB, NASB, and NIV), which I believe will better reveal these naturally occurring divisions in the text.

A Rebellious Nation: Chapters 1–12

The rebellious chosen nation is to be chastised by Yahweh, who uses surrounding nations as a tool of discipline.

We learn of Isaiah's call to preach to a rebellious nation and his divine political advice to King Ahaz. Through many failed attempts, Isaiah warns his people of the impending judgment upon the land.

Despite the current rebellion, there is a bright future for a faithful remnant of Israel; all nations will flow to Jerusalem through the son of David who will restore all things.

Prophecies to Surrounding Nations: Chapters 13–23

The following section is probably the most difficult to read because it contains prophecies to nations existing in Isaiah's day. Nonetheless, the message is a rather simple one, forming alliances with other nations will never save Israel—only God will! Here we are reminded of the fate of the surrounding nations of Judah with a series of incredible prophecies, most of which came true in world history.

The nations Isaiah addresses in this section are as follows: Babylon (1), Assyria (2), Philistia (3), Moab (4), Syria-Israeli alliance (5), Cush (6), Egypt (7), Medo-Persian defeat of Babylon (8), Edom (9), Arabia (10), Jerusalem (11), Tyre (12).

Little Apocalypse: Chapters 24–27

In this next section, Isaiah's panoramic lens makes a dramatic shift. His perspective is not focused on nations of his day but rather on the distant future—"zooming out" toward the end of human existence.

We are told of fantastical worlds where the wicked are judged, the earth is destroyed, and God's people from all over the world rejoice in their redemption. We hear songs of praise to Yahweh from all over the globe and a banquet of celebration as a result of these judgments.

The following themes are scattered throughout this section:

- the resurrection of the dead.
- supernatural protection of the righteous.
  - the birth pangs of the righteous as they wait expectantly for the judgments of God while finding refuge and protection in a secure location.
- Israel as a blessing to the whole earth.
- God's war against Satan.
- Satan and other wicked rulers' imprisonment.
  - nations hostile to Israel will come to Jerusalem to worship the Jewish God.
- the earth's destruction.
- God wiping away tears of the righteous.

Useless Alliances: Chapters 28–33

In this section we have another shift in perspective and are again looking at local nations contemporary to Isaiah with an emphasis on Egypt and Assyria.

Additionally, the section contains a series of woes toward Ephraim (Northern Kingdom) and Judah (Southern Kingdom). Isaiah predicts that Ephraim is to be captured and Judah is to be punished severely for making alliances with Egypt. Nonetheless, Isaiah states that eventually Judah will be redeemed and its enemies scattered.

Assyria's demise at Jerusalem will not be by human hands and Egypt's will be due to a hailstorm.

Eschatological Poetry—Righteous and Wicked Compared: Chapters 34–35

In chapters 34–35, Isaiah shifts his perspective again with the inclusion of poetry surrounding the Day of the Lord from the vantage point of the wicked (Isaiah 34) and the righteous (Isaiah 35). In many ways, this section serves as a conclusion to the entire book. Though they are experiencing troubles, a glorious future awaits the people of Israel—a glimmer of hope is there in the dark scenery of Isaiah's first half.

We learn that one day the impending judgment on Edom—Esau's rebellious descendents[5]—will also be released on all nations.

Yet in stark contrast, God will save Jerusalem with joy; the ransomed of the Lord shall return to Zion with singing and gladness.

Historical Interlude: Chapters 36–39

This section contains an entirely different part of Isaiah's volume, focusing on a collection of historical narratives surrounding King Hezekiah and the Assyrian threat.

In chapters 36–37, we have the miraculous account of how Judah survived a most ominous threat from the mighty Assyrian empire—the world's greatest superpower at the time. Nonetheless, Isaiah predicts that the Assyrians will not defeat Judah, and Judah's defense from this nation will not be furnished by human hands.

The biblical narrative tells us that overnight the angel of the Lord went out and slaughtered the Assyrian army just as Isaiah had predicted. This account is also found in other parts of scripture (2 Kings 20; 2 Chronicles 32).

In chapters 38–39, we learn of Hezekiah's severe illness and imminent death. The king is devastated, pleading with the Lord to remove his infirmity. The Lord answers his prayer through the prophet Isaiah; Hezekiah's life is to be extended by fifteen years, and the Lord will defend Judah from the Assyrian threat.

Isaiah uses this narrative as a transition in introducing his nation's next great threat—Babylon.

As word of Hezekiah's recovery gets out, "friendly" messengers from Babylon visit Judah, presenting gifts of condolences for his recovery. Persuaded by their hospitality, Hezekiah shows these messengers the storehouses of Judah's riches. Upon hearing this news, Isaiah predicts that everything he has shown them will be taken to Babylon, and the people will be captured by the Babylonians.

Comforting the Exiled: Chapters 40–53

The tone in chapter 40 takes a significant shift. Here Isaiah writes to a generation in exile, offering words of comfort by urging them to get a view of who their God is. He reminds them that their oppressors are but mortals, and their gods (idols and graven images) are useless, as "There is no other God but Yahweh."

Despite Israel's rebellion, God still chooses Israel, and the nation will be set free from exile in Babylon through a man named Cyrus.

Though Jacob—God's servant—was blind and useless, she is contrasted with a servant who is wise and will accomplish Israel's purpose; a servant who will suffer tremendously, in whose teachings the nations will put their hope, finding forgiveness and healing. (More is said about the identity of this servant in chapter 6, *Identifying the Lord's Servant*.)

God's Salvation : Chapters 54–62

The next section in the second half, chapters 54–62, seeks to explain what has just occurred in the death of the Suffering Servant. One key phrase that stands out is the word "salvation," mentioned *eight times* in this part. The nation of Israel is personified as a barren wife; following the death of the Suffering Servant, she will be married to God himself and have offspring that will possess the nations.

God's Redemption and Justice: Chapters 63–66

Suddenly, in chapter 63, the theme changes once again. Previously, Isaiah's message focused on providing "comfort" and "good news" of salvation, now, Isaiah focuses on the Lord's promise to reestablish Jerusalem as a glorious city never to be destroyed again. He begins with the prominent question, "Who is this trampling on the winepress with garments dipped in blood?", which leads to the creation of "new heavens and a new earth," a place where global peace and harmony are established forever.

STRUCTURAL SIMILARITIES

CHAPTER TWO

Holding this general outline of Isaiah's volume in our minds, we can now begin drawing parallels to the *books of the Bible*.

Length: Comprised of 66 units

The first similarity one encounters is that both are comprised of 66 units.

As mentioned previously, though the original scrolls (manuscripts) of scripture did not include chapters or verse numbers, ironically, Isaiah has been divided into 66 chapters. These divisions were added long after its writing, around the 1400s.[1]

This is similar to most copies of the Bible in circulation today, which contain a total of 66 books.

Since there is some dispute on which books should be included in the canon, let's take a quick detour to illustrate how this number was derived. (This aside may be skipped, if no further convincing is needed.)

Old Testament Canon: 39 Books

Beginning with the Hebrew Old Testament (TaNaKh), the first-century Jewish historian Flavius Josephus will help us shed some light on how these books were divided early on.

> For we have not an innumerable multitude of books among us, disagreeing from and contradicting one another [as the Greeks have], but only twenty-two books, which contain all the records of all the past times; which are justly believed to be divine; and of them five belong to Moses, which contain his laws and the traditions of the origin of mankind till his death ... the prophets, who were after Moses, wrote down what was done in their times in thirteen books. The remaining four books contain hymns to God, and precepts for the conduct of human life.[2]

Here, on record, is one of the earliest statements on the structure of Jewish scripture (circa AD 66). The excerpt is significant in that Josephus provides a count and general outline from a very early date—one that, as we shall see, agrees with modern copies available to us today.

Notice carefully his mention of a tripartite structure in the Jewish scriptures, which is incidentally where the word *TaNaKh* comes from — a division consisting of the Teachings (Torah), Prophecies (Nevi'im), and Writings (Ketuvim); a structure still present in today's modern Hebrew Bible.

Further support for this arrangement is also found in the Gospel of Luke, where Jesus alludes to this familiar tripartite structure, claiming that it was written about him.

> Then He said to them, "These are the words which I spoke to you while I was still with you, that all things must be fulfilled which were written in the Law of Moses and the Prophets and the Psalms concerning Me." (Luke 24:44)

So why does Josephus mention 22 books in the excerpt above, yet, today's copies of the Old Testament contain 39 books?

To help illustrate this conundrum, consider the diagram below:

	A	B	C
Torah			
1	Genesis	Genesis	Genesis
2	Exodus	Exodus	Exodus
3	Leviticus	Leviticus	Leviticus
4	Numbers	Numbers	Numbers
5	Deuteronomy	Deuteronomy	Deuteronomy
Prophets			
6	Joshua	Joshua	Joshua
7	Judges	Judges	Judges-Ruth
8	I Samuel	*Samuel*	*Samuel*
9	II Samuel	*Kings*	*Kings*
10	I Kings	Isaiah	Isaiah
11	II Kings	Jeremiah	Jeremiah-Lamentations
12	Isaiah	Ezekiel	Ezekiel
13	Jeremiah	The Twelve	The Twelve
14	Ezekiel	**Writings**	**Writings**
		Psalms	Psalms
15	Hosea	Proverbs	Proverbs
16	Joel	Job	Job
17	Amos	Song of Songs	Song of Songs
18	Obadiah	Ruth	Ecclesiastes
19	Jonah	Lamentations	Esther
20	Micah	Ecclesiastes	Daniel
21	Nahum	Esther	*Ezra-Nehemiah*
22	Habakkuk	Daniel	*Chronicles*
23	Zephaniah	*Ezra-Nehemiah*	
24	Haggai	*Chronicles*	
25	Zechariah		
26	Malachi		
Writings			
27	Psalms		
28	Proverbs		
29	Job		
30	Song of Songs		
31	Ruth		
32	Lamentations		
33	Ecclesiastes		
34	Esther		
35	Daniel		
36	Ezra		
37	Nehemiah		
38	I Chronicles		
39	II Chronicles		

Fig. 2.1: Old Testament Organization Schemes

As observed above (Fig. 2.1), the disparity with Josephus's count of 22 can be explained through the following reorganization and combining of related books. First, oftentimes the books of 1 and 2 Samuel, 1 and 2 Kings, and 1 and 2 Chronicles were combined into a single unit. Next, the twelve minor prophets (Hosea, Amos, etc., ..., through Malachi,) were condensed into one book. Finally, the books of Judges and Ruth are combined (both cover the same time period and are believed to have been written by Samuel the prophet), and similarly Lamentations is combined with Jeremiah (both believed to have been written by Jeremiah). By using different combinations of the aforementioned rules, various compilation methods have produced Old Testament copies organized into 22, 24, and 39 books.

Nonetheless, today the standard division among modern Jewish and Christian texts is most commonly for 39 books.[3]

What about the Apocrypha?

The writings known as the Apocrypha—collected from Greek manuscripts—were never accepted by the Jewish nation as (inspired) scripture; these were written in another language, time, and place. Though the concept of the Old Testament *canon* predated the Egyptian exile, some scholars believe that the Council of Jamnia had the intent of reconfirming the books to be considered canonical in light of the tumultuous state of the Jewish nation during that era.[4]

Further, though apocryphal writings already existed prior to their time, none of the New Testament writers (i.e., Paul, James, Peter, etc.) mention any of them in their accounts or claim that the scriptures in their possession were corrupt or missing in any way. Rather, they unanimously agreed to their completeness.

> Every Scripture is God-breathed and profitable for teaching, for reproof, for correction, and for instruction in righteousness, that the man of God may be complete, thoroughly equipped for every good work. (2 Timothy 3:16–17 WEB)

New Testament Canon: 27 Books

When it comes to the New Testament books, though there are several schools of thought on the nature, process, and even definition of canonization, most would agree that between the second and fourth centuries the collection of authoritative writings had reached full maturation, enjoying widespread consensus within the early church community.[5]

Early Statements on Individual Books

By the early second century, we have on record a plethora of statements with regard to the authoritativeness of individual books from many of the apostolic fathers (i.e., Ignatius of Antioch, Irenaeus of Lyons, Clement of Alexandria, Origen, etc.), many of whom were closely discipled by or in community with the original apostles of Christ.[6]

For instance, in his famous work *Adversus haereses* (180 AD), Irenaeus of Lyons includes references to many of the New Testament books. Most remarkably, for this date, he provides a clear defense on which books should be included in the Gospel collection—indicating that there are only four.

> The Gospels could not possibly be either more or less in number than they are. Since there are four zones of the world in which we live, and four principal winds.... From this it is clear that the Word, the artificer of all things, being manifested to men gave us the gospel, fourfold in form but held together by one Spirit.[7]

Thus, by the second century the landscape of the canonical books was mostly effectuated.

Full-List Records

One of the earliest references mentioning the entire 27-book collection comes from the pen of the theologian Athanasius of Alexandria. In the *39th Festal Letter of Athanasius* (367 CE), an annual letter to the Egyptian churches under his jurisdiction, he is motivated by the need to "set forth in order the writings that have been put in the canon," claiming that many are being led astray by "so-called" apocryphal books, written by those who were not eyewitnesses to the Gospel events. In this letter, he provides a full-list of these divine books.

> Again, it is not tedious to speak of the books of the New Testament. These are: the four Gospels, according to Matthew, Mark, Luke, and John. After these, The Acts of the Apostles, and the seven epistles called Catholic: of James, one; of Peter, two, of John, three; after these, one of Jude. In addition, there are fourteen epistles of Paul the apostle, written in this order: the first, to the Romans; then, two to the Corinthians; after these, to the Galatians; next, to the Ephesians, then, to the Philippians; then, to the Colossians; after these, two to the Thessalonians; and that to the Hebrews; and again, two to Timothy; one to Titus; and lastly, that to Philemon. And besides, the Revelation of John .... In these alone the teaching of godliness is proclaimed. Let no one add to these; let nothing be taken away from them.[8] *Athanasius, (Thirty-Ninth Festal Letter of AD 367)*

What about the Gnostic Writings?

With statements such as the two aforementioned (Irenaeus and Athanasius), we can establish quite confidently the status of the New Testament canon, even just a short-time from the original events.

From these records, it becomes evident how the rise of Gnosticism and Marcionism provided further impetus for these written statements in identifying which books were to be considered part of scriptures, effectively defending orthodox Christianity from such heretical teachings. This is clearly stated in the introduction of *Adversus haereses* as Irenaeus's motive for writing, which is subtitled *On the Detection and Overthrow of the So-Called Gnosis*.

According to Irenaeus, these writings contain a number of theological inconsistencies that were not in keeping with the (then hundred-year-old) doctrines passed directly from the apostles of Christ and were consequently rejected by key ecclesiastical leadership for inclusion in scripture.

His volume is also significant in that he not only provides positive affirmation of authoritative books but also refers to certain works and declares them heretical. Below are some examples of Irenaeus and his denunciations of two works; the Gospel of Truth and the Gospel of Judas:

> But the followers of Valentinus, putting away all fear, bring forward their own compositions and boast that they have more Gospels than really exist. Indeed their audacity has gone so far that they entitle their recent composition the Gospel of Truth, though it agrees in nothing with the Gospels of the apostles, and so no Gospel of theirs is free from blasphemy. For if what they produce is the Gospel of Truth, and is different from those which the apostles handed down to us, those who care to can learn how it can be show from the Scriptures themselves that [then] what is handed down from the apostles is *not the Gospel of Truth*. (3.11.9) [9]

> Others again declare that Cain derived his being from the Power above, and acknowledge that Esau, Korah, the Sodomites, and all such persons, are related to themselves. On this account, they add, they have been assailed by the Creator, yet no one of them has suffered injury. For Sophia was in the habit of carrying off that which belonged to her from them to herself. They declare that Judas the traitor was thoroughly acquainted with these things, and that he alone, knowing the truth as no others did, accomplished the

mystery of the betrayal; by him all things, both earthly and heavenly, were thus thrown into confusion. They produce a fictitious history of this kind, which they style the *Gospel of Judas*. (1.31.1)[10]

How Were These Books Determined?

Based on a survey of various perspectives (definitions) on canonization, one New Testament scholar, Dr. Michael Kruger, has compiled a list of criteria—which in many ways is a harmonization of "competing" points of view—that books must meet in order to be considered canonical.

Below are some of these criteria, which he calls "Attributes of Canonicity,"[11] as seen in his work *Canon Revisited*:

1. Divine Qualities:
   The book should be Orthodox in its teaching, in agreement with the teachings of the thriving church from the apostolic era—a period when there were still an abundance of living witnesses and direct disciples of the apostles.

2. Apostolic Origins:
   It must be written by one of the apostles alive during the time of Jesus—or a close associate.

3. Corporate Reception
   Furthermore, the work needed to have global acceptance by the early community of Christians—ecclesiastical consensus; it must be widely received by the corporate Church, who understood the authority of these writings to be on par with that of Old Testament scriptures.

By applying these criteria, together with the statements of the early apostolic leaders, we begin to get a picture (though very brief) of the origins of the twenty-seven book New Testament canon in our possession.

Nonetheless, for our purposes here, suffice it to say that when combined (Old and New Testaments), the books of the Bible contain a total of 66 books, which is incidentally also the number of chapters in Isaiah.

Halved at 40

The next anomaly is not only that both Isaiah and *the Books of the Bible* have been halved at 40; but that the themes, content, and time coverage of both halves appear to be rather identical.

It is regularly known by scholars and students of Isaiah that there are two distinct halves to the book—so markedly that it has led many to believe that there was a second (anonymous) author responsible for the second half, oftentimes called "Deutero-Isaiah," or "Second Isaiah."[12]

One of the main arguments that proponents of this view recount is that this drastic shift in theme and perspective can *only* mean the contributions of another writer. Much more is said on the authorship of Isaiah in the *Appendix – A Question of Authorship: Did More than One Person Write Isaiah?* Nonetheless, at this point, simply mentioning the controversy suffices in demonstrating the division of Isaiah into two halves occurring at chapter 40.

OLD TESTAMENT PARALLELS

CHAPTER THREE

Themes and Messages of the First Half

The content and themes of the Old Testament are all found in the first half, many times, in the same order.¹

As we have seen, this section of Isaiah contains a collection of prophecies that jump back and forth in scope from Isaiah's present day to the end of human history. Metaphorically speaking, with a microscope he offers a contemporaneous examination of his nation-state, uncovering their rebellious habits, hidden woes, and shortcomings; with a telescope he is able to look into the future of his nation offering encouraging words about a day when Israel becomes a world empire never to be extinguished.

This collection (song, narrative, prophecy, judgment etc.) contains similar categories and can almost be mapped to exact books or sections of the Old Testament, which has the following distribution: Torah (5 books), prophecy (21 books), writings (13 books).

In the next section, we will proceed by mapping sections in Isaiah's volume to a corresponding type of writing in the *Old Testament*.

Similarities to the Teachings (Torah)

Rebellious Children

The first section of Isaiah begins with the rebellion of God's children, as evidenced in passages such as this: "I have nourished and brought up children, and they have rebelled against Me" (Isaiah 1:2). Similarly, in chapters 1 and 3, Isaiah compares his nation to Sodom and Gomorrah.

The tribe of Judah (now inhabiting Jerusalem)—God's faithful people—who once lived in the bliss of prosperity after the reign of King David, have at this point lost their "paradise" and, based on Isaiah's prophecies, are about to lose their land.

Isaiah goes on to provide a national critique on the shortcomings of their worship, describing as well their sins and disobedience.

The same theme of humanity's rebellion occurs at the beginning of Torah, where the scriptures tell us of the fall of man and how the fellowship in the garden was ruined through the sin of mankind. Additionally, these books go on to recount this nation's continued downward spiral, covering the events of Israel's wandering through the desert all the way through to the death of Moses.

A Righteous Prophet and His family

Starting with the book of Exodus, God raises up Moses (a righteous man) to be a voice to the Israelites.

In the same fashion we observe the prophet himself, Isaiah, wrestling with God's people taking on the role of mediator between God and the people. We learn of Isaiah's family through mentions of his wife and two sons (Shear-Jashub, Mahershalalhasbaz), who are to be prophetic signs for the people. Eventually, Isaiah predicts that their rebellion will lead them into captivity.

> Therefore my people have gone into captivity,
> Because they have no knowledge;
> Their honorable men are famished,
> And their multitude dried up with thirst. (Isa 5:13)

This seems to parallel the accounts of Moses who, like Isaiah, pleads with God's people to no avail—his message falls on deaf ears. In Deuteronomy 27–32, Moses similarly predicts Israel's failure to obey and further exile in Egypt.

Both Works Contain Two Songs in This Section

In this section of Isaiah there are two songs, the first in chapter 5 and the other in chapter 12. This is also paralleled in the *Torah*, where Moses includes two songs; the first at the crossing of the Red Sea (Exodus 15) and the other at the end of his life (Deuteronomy 32).

Glimpses of Redemption

At the garden, we learn of God's answer to humanity's downward spiral resulting from Adam's sin.

A new kind of human is needed to restore the earth, and through the seed of Eve the serpent will be crushed. As we continue reading, we learn that the promise of redemption is to come through the family of Abraham, where they will eventually return to their land and be blessed.

Similarly, in this section, Isaiah provides increasingly detailed glimpses of a coming Messiah; God's answer to Israel's rebellion. These accounts are sprinkled around his messages of rebuke and impending judgment.

For instance, in chapter 4, the first mention of a certain character is made: *the Branch of the Lord*; he will be glorious, and they will have safety from the storm.

Furthermore, we learn that a son to be born will become an everlasting father; that a king from the lineage of David is to bring forth world peace and governance; that a shoot from Jesse will judge between the nations and settle disputes; that the cobra and the child will play together; and that all nations will come up to Zion to worship the Jewish God.

The themes of Torah can be seen scattered in these sections, as in the depiction of Israel as a rebellious nation and God's promises to Abraham to restore his people.

Similarities to the Prophets (Nevi'im)

The Nevi'im can be subdivided into two distinct sections. These are the "former prophets"—which include books like: Joshua, Judges, Samuel, and Kings—and the "latter prophets"—which can then be further subdivided into the major prophets (Isaiah, Jeremiah, and Ezekiel) and minor prophets (Hosea, Joel, Amos, Obadiah, Jonah, Micah, Nahum, Habakkuk, Zephaniah, Haggai, Zechariah, and Malachi).

A similar organizational scheme occurs in this section of Isaiah with the difference that the two sections have been reversed in order.

Isaiah and the Latter Prophets

Recall that in chapters 13–23, the text contains short prophecies given to twelve different nations, followed by a collection of prophecies concerning the whole world at the end of human history (chapters 24–27). This can be compared to the latter prophets containing the twelve minor prophets and the three major prophets.

Isaiah and the Former Prophets

Then again, in chapters 28–33, Isaiah changes his perspective and includes prophecies to local contemporary nations of his day; including Egypt and Assyria. His focus here shifts within the nation of Israel and includes mostly bad news to the ten tribes (though there are a few mentions of a righteous remnant of Israel).

Similarities to the Writings (Ketuvim)

This section of the Tanakh contains a diverse collection of scrolls taking the form of poetry and historical narratives covering relatively late events of the Babylonian Captivity. The exact ordering of these books was never finalized in the Jewish tradition, and they are ordered differently in various compilations.[2] This section can also parallel the writings of Isaiah in chapters 34–39.

Poetic Books

First, chapters 34–35 of Isaiah contain writings that really stand out from the rest of this section as they are very poetic; many of which are written in the form of a song. The text suggests that Isaiah himself was a musician, as evidenced in phrases such as "I will sing a song about my beloved's vineyard," which is essentially a sermon-song written as a metaphor of the nation of Israel (Isaiah 5).

Chapter 34 focuses on the day of vengeance from the perspective of those hostile to Israel, and therefore takes on a more somber tone. In stark contrast, chapter 35 focuses on the day of vengeance from the perspective of the righteous and is filled with exuberance and praise.

> And the ransomed of the LORD shall return,
> And come to Zion with singing,
> With everlasting joy on their heads.
> They shall obtain joy and gladness,
> And sorrow and sighing shall flee away. (Isa 35:10)

We can see the similarities here to books like Psalms, Ecclesiastes, and the Song of Solomon.

Babylonian Narratives

Following this poetic interlude, Isaiah goes on with a historical narrative concerning the life of King Hezekiah. Suddenly, a new nation is mentioned here and given greater attention—Babylon.

Where previously in this section the biggest threat was Assyria, here he predicts Judah's eventual captivity by the Babylonians.

Similarly at the end of the Tanakh, in the Ketuvim we see tales of specific characters in Babylon (Daniel, Esther, Ruth, etc.), stories which can parallel Isaiah's narrative on King Hezekiah and the visitors from Babylon.

NEW TESTAMENT PARALLELS

CHAPTER FOUR

Themes and Structure of the Second Half

As mentioned previously, the fortieth chapter of Isaiah marks a significant thematic shift in the book. Where previously the topics centered (mostly) on disciplinary judgment of Israel and surrounding nations, the chapter 40 begins in a much more optimistic mood, evident in the words "Comfort, comfort ye my people." There is almost a reintroduction of vocabulary here with terms such as *salvation*, *redemption*, and *Herald of Good News* used repeatedly in this section, which incidentally are absent in the first half and even scarcer in other books of the Old Testament (e.g., *good news* is used eight times in the second half but completely absent in the first).

Similarly, in the books of the Bible, the fortieth book in the collection marks a significant thematic shift, transitioning from the Old Testament into the Gospels of the New Testament. Incidentally, the term *gospel* originates from the Greek word *evangelio*, meaning "good news."

Another interesting parallel from this section is that the words of Isaiah 40 have been quoted directly at the beginning of the Gospels, "the voice crying out in the wilderness," and attributed to John the Baptist, who prepares the way for the arrival of Jesus. Isaiah 42:1 is also quoted of Jesus during his baptism, "My beloved son in whom I delight."

Drawing further parallels to the *New Testament*, recall that this part of Isaiah can be subdivided into the following three sections: Comfort and Atonement (chapters 40–53), Salvation (54–59), and Future Glory (60–66).

In the same fashion, we notice that the New Testament contains three clear sections grouped by type of writing: Gospels, Letters, and Prophecy.

Let's dig a little deeper in comparing chapters 40–66 of Isaiah to the New Testament.

Similarities to the Gospels

Four Gospels and Servant Songs

We begin by examining this first third of the second half. Immediately we notice, in the section containing chapters 40–53, the introduction of a mysterious figure known as *My Servant* or *The Servant of Yahweh.*

In the Hebrew text there are four identifiable sections that break the narrative in the surrounding text and take on the form of Hebrew songs, focusing on this one character. They can be found in the following sections:

1. Isaiah 42:1–4
2. Isaiah 49:1–6
3. Isaiah 50:4–9
4. Isaiah 52:13–53:12

These Servant Songs, as they are popularly called, provide some rather interesting details about this Servant from various angles. The message of these Servant Songs can be summarized respectively as follows:

1. He will bring forth justice on the earth.
2. Through his life he will rescue both Jew and Gentile.
3. He will be afflicted and disgraced.

4. Though he is to suffer an agonizing death for the sins of my people, he will come back to life and see his offspring possess the earth.

Similarly, in the *four* gospels of "good news," the New Testament provides *four* different accounts of the life, ministry, and crucifixion of Jesus in the books of Mark, Matthew, Luke, and John.

John and Affliction in the 4th Song

Just as the Gospel of John is somewhat distinct from the other three (the synoptic) gospels, providing the most graphic portrayal of the crucifixion; so the fourth Servant Song also seems to stand out, providing the most gruesome account of the death of the Suffering Servant, which is to serve as atonement for "my people" and for "many nations."

> Just as many were astonished at you,
> So His visage was marred more than any man,
> And His form more than the sons of men. (Isa 52:14)
>
> Yet we esteemed Him stricken,
> Smitten by God, and afflicted ...
> But He was wounded for our transgressions,
> He was bruised for our iniquities. (Isa 53:4–5)

(See Chapter 6, *Identifying the Lord's Servant*, for more on this servant.)

Similarities to the Letters

The next section of Isaiah, chapters 54–62, seeks to explain what has just occurred in the death of the Suffering Servant. As we noted previously, one of the keywords that stands out here is the word *salvation*, occurring eight times in this part. The nation of Israel is personified as a barren wife; following the death of the Suffering Servant, she will be married to God himself and have offspring that will possess the nations.

This is paralleled in the book of Acts and the Epistles (letters) written to the newly emerging churches after the death and resurrection of Jesus. Many of Paul's letters focus on explaining how that event should transform their lives; he covers a myriad of topics such as instructions for orderly worship and doctrine.

The Multiplication of the Church and the Barren Woman

The first similarity is that immediately after the death of the Servant, Isaiah tells us that God's wife—personified as a barren woman—is about to experience multiplication. She is told,

> Enlarge the place of your tent,
> And let them stretch out the curtains of your dwellings.
> (Isa 54:2)

The reason is that the Lord will be her husband, and her offspring will spread throughout the nations.

Similarly, in the book of Acts we have the historical record of the birth and expansion of the church. We are given an explanation of how this new movement, originating with twelve ordinary Jewish men, reaches to the ends of the earth. Paul even references the husband–wife metaphor in several of his letters as a picture of God's relationship with his righteous people.

> I am jealous for you with godly jealousy. For I have betrothed you to one husband, that I may present you as a chaste virgin to Christ. (2 Corinthians 11:2)

Both of these accounts are centered around God's bride and the multiplication after the death of a prominent figure.

Cyrus and Paul Compared

In the second half of Isaiah, we have several mentions of a man named Cyrus—a special "shepherd" of God who is called by name to rescue the Israelites out of Babylon. There are several striking similarities to the apostle Paul.

At first, both men were hostile to the people of God. For instance, Cyrus the Great was a Medo-Persian ruler who as a non-Jew was initially hostile to the Jewish nation.[1] However, when he reached Babylon in his conquest, he allowed the Jews to return to their homeland and rebuild the temple.[2] He is perhaps the most notable figure of the Babylonian Exile, without which the chosen nation might possibly not have survived.

Similarly, Saul of Tarsus (Paul) was initially a persecutor of the church and saw the movement of Jesus followers as a threat to Judaism. Eventually, he turns out to be one of the most notable figures, responsible for writing nearly a third of the New Testament, the letters. It is speculated that the Gospel of Luke and Acts, addressed to Theophilus, were initially written with the intent of providing a defense for Paul's release from prison.[3]

Cyrus the Great was called by name before birth; Paul the apostle was called and set apart through a direct encounter with the risen Jesus.

Instructions on Spiritual Disciplines

Continuing through this section, Isaiah includes a critique on spiritual disciplines (such as in chapter 58) by providing instructions on the topics of fasting, the Sabbath, and festivals.

Similarly, many of the New Testament letters also provide specific instructions on orderly worship and conduct in this newly emerging movement of Jesus followers.

For instance, consider the similarities of these passages, where both James and Isaiah make statements on the futility of religion that does not consider those who are less fortunate.

> Is it not to share your bread with the hungry and bring the homeless poor into your house; when you see the naked, to cover him, and not to hide yourself from your own flesh? (Isa 58:7 ESV)

> Religion that is pure and undefiled before God the Father is this: to visit orphans and widows in their affliction, and to keep oneself unstained from the world. (James 1:27 ESV)

Gentiles Welcomed

Continuing to draw parallels in this section of Isaiah, we notice a rare invitation offered to non-Jews.

Traditionally, gentiles and eunuchs were excluded from Jewish worship. However, during times of captivity, many Gentiles became curious about Jewish worship—even participating with Jews in these religious ceremonies.[4] Isaiah extends an invitation to these foreigners, who will be allowed to participate in worship of the Hebrew God with the condition that they can keep the Sabbath and abstain from swine.

> Let not the foreigner who has joined himself to the
> Lord say,
> "The Lord will surely separate me from his people";
> and let not the eunuch say,
> "Behold, I am a dry tree."
> For thus says the Lord: ...
> "And the foreigners who join themselves to the Lord,
> to minister to him, to love the name of the Lord,
> and to be his servants,
> everyone who keeps the Sabbath and does not profane it,
> and holds fast my covenant—
> these I will bring to my holy mountain,
> and make them joyful in my house of prayer;
> their burnt offerings and their sacrifices
> will be accepted on my altar;
> for my house shall be called a house of prayer
> for all peoples." (Isa 56:3–7 ESV)

In a similar fashion, Paul, after facing some frustrations in preaching to the Jewish nation, began to focus his attention on reaching Gentiles. At first, there was considerable debate and confusion as to whether Gentiles should be allowed to participate in this newly emerging movement originating from Judaism.

Yet, in his letters, Paul reasoned that if Gentiles were also being filled with the Holy Spirit, then salvation must be extended to non-Jews as well, and concluded that the gospel is "first for the Jew then for the Gentile" (Romans 1:16 NIV).

The Prominence of the Holy Spirit

Finally, the Spirit being "poured out" is mentioned four times in this section; such as in the famous lines quoted by Jesus in Isaiah 61:1, "the Spirit of the Lord is upon me," and "My covenant with them: My Spirit who is upon you" (Isaiah 59:21).

Additionally, phrases like "grieving the Holy Spirit," which was later borrowed by New Testament writers, originates from this section of Isaiah.

Similarities to Revelation

Finally, we arrive at the last section of both works.

The final book of the Bible is quite different from the letters we have seen in previous sections of the New Testament. It is the grand climax of God's story, culminating in the Revelation of Jesus Christ, who will judge the nations and have the kingdoms of the earth come under his sway.

In it we have an unparalleled description of God's plan to restore the earth and establish a new government in the New Heavens and New Earth. While this theme is not new to the scriptures, the book of Revelation is by far the most detailed and is written as a firsthand witness to these events.

Surprisingly, in this last section of Isaiah, chapters 63–66, we find the same themes sprinkled throughout. Isaiah ends his prophecy on a most triumphant note: God will restore Jerusalem and defend them from their enemies, and all the nations will come to worship the Jewish God. He also includes a reference to the New Heavens and New Earth, a place of rest and world peace.

Many of God's righteous people will experience protection and be filled with joy, while the wicked will be in anguish, similar to the plagues of Egypt during the time of Moses. This is why many times throughout scripture these events are called "The Great and Terrible Day" (Joel 2:11).

Let's explore the similarities between these two sections a little more closely. We begin first with the "bad news," the story told from the perspective of the wicked (those who refuse to repent even after repeated opportunities).

The Terrible Day

Both Isaiah and Revelation tell us how those hostile to Yahweh will experience these events: despite all the signs, the wicked still love their evil doings and refuse to turn from their ways.

A Day of Vengeance – the Sound of Recompense

In Revelation, we have repeated mentions of Jesus coming to render justice on all wickedness as evidenced in phrases such as "Hide us from the terror." We are told that out of his mouth comes a sharp two-edged sword.

Similarly, Isaiah mentions that as Jerusalem is reestablished, it will be through the voice of the Lord; he comes with fire to render rebuke on Israel's enemies.

> The sound of noise from the city!
> A voice from the temple!
> The voice of the LORD,
> Who fully repays His enemies! (Isa 66:6)

The Avenger Dipped in Blood

Apart from those who encountered the risen Jesus, most remember him as the defeated rabbi hanging helplessly on the cross.

The scriptures tell us that at his second "appearing," he is coming as a man of war, a military leader; the Lion of the Tribe of Judah will come to exterminate wickedness and restore peace on earth. We are given a brief glimpse of him whose eyes are blazing with fire as he leads a multinational army against "the Beast" and "the False Witness." John, in Revelation, tells us that he has a robe dipped in blood.

> Now I saw heaven opened, and behold, a white horse. And He who sat on him was called Faithful and True, and in righteousness He judges and makes war. His eyes were like a flame of fire, and on His head were many crowns. He had a name written that no one knew except Himself. He was clothed with a *robe dipped in blood*, and His name is called The Word of God. (Revelation 19:11–13)

This description of Jesus is not unique to Revelation. Similarly, the prophet Isaiah, in beginning to describe the restoration of Jerusalem, sees a mysterious figure coming from Edom to wage war against God's enemies. This figure is also filled with "garments dipped in blood."

> I have trodden the winepress alone,
> And from the peoples no one was with Me.
> For I have trodden them in My anger,
> And trampled them in My fury;
> Their *blood is sprinkled* upon My garments,
> And I have *stained all My robes*.
> For the day of vengeance is in My heart,
> And the year of My redeemed has come. (Isa 63:3–4, italics added)

Return of the Plagues of Egypt

The events described in Revelation are many times compared to the plagues of Egypt released upon Pharaoh. Here, however, they are released on the Antichrist and his cohorts.

Similarly, in Isaiah's depiction of this mysterious figure from Edom, he mentions that these events reminded the people of the great feats during the liberation of the Jews in Egypt.

> Then he remembered the days of old, Moses and his people, saying: "Where is He who brought them up out of the sea With the shepherd of His flock? Where is He who put His Holy Spirit within them, Who led them by the right hand of Moses, With His glorious arm, Dividing the water before them To make for Himself an everlasting name." (Isa 63:11–12)

Thus, as we approach the end of both works, we are told how the wicked will perceive these events leading to the establishment of New Heavens and a New Earth. Both even mention the sight of dead bodies being exposed publicly before all nations, bloodshed covering a third of the oceans as is mentioned by Isaiah through great supernatural events like the plagues of Egypt during the time of Moses.

Great Day

Now we explore how these events will be experienced by the righteous. The scriptures tell us that believers and followers of Yahweh look forward to this day with great expectation. It is a day of justice. Isaiah tells us that he hears the voice of the LORD rendering recompense on all that is high and lofty.

Bridegroom Imagery

Like any good romantic tale, the grand crescendo of the Bible's story is leading us to a great wedding, followed by a great feast. This is alluded to throughout the scriptures, but Revelation gives us the greatest detail of this wedding procession.

> "Let us be glad and rejoice and give Him glory, for the marriage of the Lamb has come, and His wife has made herself ready." And to her it was granted to be arrayed in fine linen, clean and bright, for the fine linen is the righteous acts of the saints. (Revelation 19:7–8)

Similarly, Isaiah uses this bridal language in the midst of this section to describe these events.

> For as a young man marries a virgin, So shall your sons marry you; And as the bridegroom rejoices over the bride, So shall your God rejoice over you. (Isa 62:5)

The Spirit and the Bride say, "Come!"

In both sections we are told that God's followers are pleading for the return of God to liberate them from their present circumstances.

In Revelation 6, right after the fifth seal is released, we have a sight of God's followers pleading for God's justice.

> And they cried with a loud voice, saying, "How long, O Lord, holy and true, until You judge and avenge our blood on those who dwell on the earth?" (Revelation 6:10)

Compare this to Isaiah 63, where similarly, Israel is pleading for God to come down and save them.

> Return for Your servants' sake, The tribes of Your inheritance .... Oh, that You would rend the heavens! That You would come down! That the mountains might shake at Your presence. (Isa 63:17; 64:1)

This essentially summarizes the cry of God's saints in Revelation, and as we saw in the previous section, they are personified as a bride with a great cry: "The Spirit and the bride say, 'Come!'" (Revelation 22:17).

Global Restoration and the New Creation

Previously in chapter 24, Isaiah mentions that at the day of judgment the earth will be utterly destroyed and laid waste.

Here, at the restoration of all things he tells us that God is going to create New Heavens and a New Earth; it is a world of universal peace, even extending into the animal kingdom.

> "The wolf and the lamb shall graze together; the lion shall eat straw like the ox, and dust shall be the serpent's food. They shall not hurt or destroy in all my holy mountain," says the LORD. (Isa 65:25 ESV)

This was mentioned previously in earlier descriptions in which a descendant from David will rise to bring about its fulfillment.

This theme is further expanded upon in the last chapter of Revelation where John also describes a world in the New Jerusalem where peace and harmony are restored—forever.

> Then I saw a new heaven and a new earth, for the first heaven and the first earth had passed away, and the sea was no more. And I saw the holy city, new Jerusalem, coming down out of heaven from God, prepared as a bride adorned for her husband. (Revelation 21:1–2 ESV)

The Lord Will Be Your Light and Gates Never Shut

In the description of the New Jerusalem, both Isaiah and Revelation have an unusual observation regarding the city's source of light. The sun and the moon will no longer be needed, as God will be its perpetual source of light. Compare the following two passages:

> The sun shall no longer be your light by day, Nor for brightness shall the moon give light to you; But the LORD will be to you an everlasting light, And your God your glory. Your sun shall no longer go down, Nor shall your moon withdraw itself; For the LORD will be your everlasting light, And the days of your mourning shall be ended. (Isa 60:19–20)

> I heard a loud voice from heaven saying, "Behold, the tabernacle of God is with men, and He will dwell with them, and they shall be His people. God Himself will be with them and be their God." (Revelation 21:3)

Furthermore, both accounts mention that these gates will never be shut. This suggests a world where crime does not exist and gates of protection are no longer needed—a world where violence shall be no more.

> Therefore your gates shall be open continually; They shall not be shut day or night, That men may bring to you the wealth of the Gentiles, And their kings in procession. (Isa 60:11)

> Its gates shall not be shut at all by day (there shall be no night there). (Revelation 21:25)

The Cluster of Grapes and Protection for His Remnant

In the midst of the carnage, the righteous will experience supernatural protection. Isaiah and Revelation use similar metaphors to illustrate God's protection of the righteous.

Recall the parable of the vineyard in Isaiah 5, "Let me sing to you a song about my beloved's vineyard," where the people of Israel are personified as a vineyard. The prophetic message is that, having become a rebellious nation, they would be destroyed since they did not produce the grapes the vinedresser was expecting.

By comparison, in the related illustration found in chapter 65, Isaiah mentions that this cluster of grapes is found to contain "juice," and consequently will be salvaged from the imminent destruction.

> As when juice is still found in a cluster of grapes
> and people say, "Don't destroy it,
> there is still a blessing in it,"
> so will I do in behalf of my servants;
> I will not destroy them all. (Isa 65:8 NIV)

A similar metaphor is used in Revelation 14:18, where God's servants are also personified as a cluster of grapes ready to be harvested before God pours out his wrath. Additionally, in Revelation 7:3, the righteous servants are spared in a similar fashion where one of the angels is about to release one of the seals of judgment but is halted until the servants of God are identified and spared.

> Another angel came out from the altar, the angel who has authority over the fire, and he called with a loud voice to the one who had the sharp sickle, "Put in your sickle and gather the clusters from the vine of the earth, for its grapes are ripe." (Revelation 14:18 ESV)

> Do not harm the earth, the sea, or the trees till we have sealed the servants of our God on their foreheads. (Revelation 7:3)

Conclusion

As we draw these parallels to a close, the similarities of Isaiah to the collection of the books of the Bible becomes something of great intrigue in light of the historical documentation demonstrating the gap in time between the publication of these two works. It seems to have been an "accident" that Isaiah's book should reflect the entire canon this closely. This thousand-year foreshadowing anomaly further leverages the feeling of transcendence found while reading Isaiah.

Given the possible subjectivity on the ordering of the books of the Bible, and the later addition of chapter and verse numbers, I submit these observations as sheer hypotheses for the reader's own investigation. If these similarities seem forced or too coincidental, readers are encouraged to explore both of these texts and form their own opinions.

Nonetheless, if anything, this observation can serve as a helpful study tool in approaching Isaiah's document; which—as we shall see in the next section, where we explore the many historical and still-future predictions—contains some unbelievable messages.

(Below is a chart that summarizes the findings of this section.)

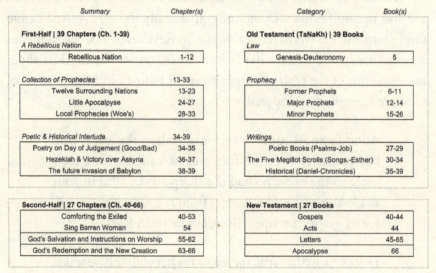

Fig. 4.1: Overview of Homologous Structures

PART 2
PANORAMIC PERSPECTIVES

BUCKET A: HISTORICAL PREDICTIONS (800 BC–1 BC)

CHAPTER FIVE

Now that we have a rough overview of the book and the themes that are discussed, let's focus on specific oracles.

Isaiah's "prophetic lens" is centered on the land of Judah at three different levels of magnification: Judah, the Fertile Crescent, and the entire globe covering three different time periods: his present day, the near future, and the distant future (extending to the end of human history). Metaphorically speaking, it's as if he uses a microscope to inspect the affairs of his local nation, making predictions that, to his contemporaries, are verifiable within one lifetime. Then with a telescope he zooms out further in time and space, stretching out to the entire globe at the end of the age.

In order to better grasp Isaiah's panoramic perspective let's arrange these predictions into three buckets: A, B, C.

Bucket A will represent predictions that were fulfilled shortly after (or during) Isaiah's lifetime, leading up to the turn of the millennium. *Bucket B* will represent predictions fulfilled in the following era, at about a thousand years after Isaiah's lifetime (in the early Christian era). *Bucket C* will represent predictions that have yet to occur, visions of days to come.

The diagram below is a rough timeline illustrating the time interval covered in each bucket:

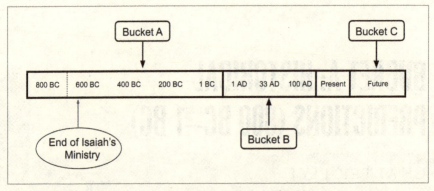

Fig. 5.1: Isaiah's Prophetic Timeline and Designation of Buckets

As we explore some of these predictions, it is important to keep certain facts in mind. Isaiah's work is not just a random collection of arbitrary sayings but—penned in the context of time and space—accounts that are historically verifiable even through other non-biblical sources of the Mesopotamian era.

The specificity and rarity of these prophecies are so remarkable that many doubt the single authorship of this book as Isaiah's.[1] How could someone know the specifics of world history centuries before? Surely, these oracles must have been written by someone else, after these events had occurred. One problem with this view, as we shall see, is that portions of the text—which even skeptics attribute to the prophet Isaiah—contain predictions extending beyond his lifetime, so proposing multiple authorship does not solve this problem: the avoidance of special revelation. (We have included a more in-depth discussion on the book's authorship in the Appendix.)

For each of the examples below, take into consideration that Isaiah's ministry began just a few years before Uzziah's death (most likely in the 740s BC) and continued until the fourteenth year of the reign of Hezekiah (who died in 698 BC). According to rabbinical commentary, tradition has it that Isaiah was martyred (sawn asunder) by King Manasses in 698 BC.[2] Thus, many of the things he wrote were not fulfilled during his lifetime; neither Isaiah nor his immediate contemporaries would be living witnesses to many of these predictions.

Another caveat to consider is that Isaiah does not always provide a precise sequential timeline for all of his prophecies; sometimes his predictions are even coupled with events from different periods in the same thought. Occasionally a time stamp or unfolding of events is provided; yet in most cases, exact chronology is absent, and it is simply stated that the event will happen *sometime* in the future.

How to Read This Section

It is not necessary to read the following sections sequentially, and can almost be treated as an almanac or encyclopedia of Isaianic prophecy. They have been sorted and organized by their dates of fulfillment, chronologically. As these prophecies are explored, you will notice a pattern where each prediction contains a brief summary; an estimated numerical calculation giving its *Time To Fulfillment* (TTF)—the elapsed time from when it is believed Isaiah gave such utterance to its fulfillment as seen documented in history; and at the end, scripture references which will be helpful in providing additional context to that prediction.

Below is a map of the Fertile Crescent (just before the turn of the eighth century BC), which can be used as a general reference as we survey the predictions in this section.

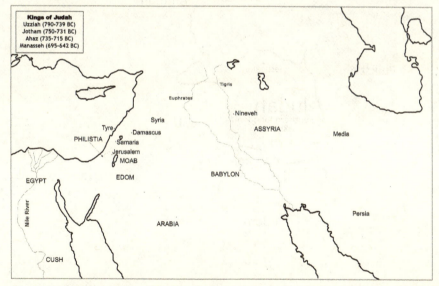

Fig. 5.2: *8th Century Map of the Fertile Crescent*

1) Immanuel, the Decline of Syria, and the Lost Tribes of Israel

Isaiah predicts the destruction of the Northern Kingdom, the demise of the Israelite–Syrian Alliance, and the unlikely survival of Judah. This was fulfilled during the Assyrian sieges of 732–676 BC, when the Syrians and the Ten Tribes in the north were taken captive and scattered throughout the Assyrian empire.

TTF = 65 years

Historical Context

Fig. 5.3: Assyrian Invasion of Israelite0150Syrian Alliance

During the transition of leadership from Jotham to Ahaz, an aggressive political alliance formed between Syria and Israel (the Northern Kingdom). The intentions were to capture Jerusalem (the Southern Kingdom of Judah), divide the wealth between the two nations, and appoint a new king.

When the news reached King Ahaz and the people of Judah, they were utterly terrified; King Ahaz's knees shook like the trees in the wind. The humble nation of Judah consisting of just two tribes (Benjamin and Judah) was now in opposition with the allied Ten Tribes of the north and the nation of Syria. The odds of survival for Judah were slim; Ahaz knew it, and so did the rest of the nation.

In the midst of this gloomy prognostic, Isaiah comforts King Ahaz with the unlikely message that in sixty-five years the Ten Tribes will no longer be a people and that he need not worry about this threat. Furthermore, in chapter 28 he predicts that Ephraim (one of the tribes in the north) will fade away.

As a further indicator of these prophecies, Isaiah declares that a sign will be given to serve as a time stamp and further confirmation of his prediction. A young woman (or virgin)[3]—most likely living in the royal palace—will have a child and call him Immanuel. Before this child reaches the age of moral accountability, Syria will be destroyed.

Many of the names of children mentioned in these chapters carry a deeper meaning. In this case *Immanuel* means "God is with us," supporting Isaiah's claim that the threat in the North will not prevail—as God is on their side.

Additionally, events in the life of Isaiah's own son Maher shalal hash baz, will also serve as a prophetic time stamp on the unfolding of these predictions.

Though there is no record on the birth of the child Immanuel, this prophecy was fulfilled during the leadership of Tiglath-Pileser III (King of Assyria) during a series of invasions from 732 to 676 BC, thus marking a sixty-five-year period, as Isaiah mentioned.[4] The Ten (Lost) Tribes of the north were scattered about the Kingdom of Assyria never to return, and as Isaiah promised Ahaz, Judah remained untouched, and he remained a living witness to the fulfillment of these words.

[Further readings: Isaiah 7–8, 17:1–14, 28]

2) Assyria Fails in Capturing Jerusalem

Isaiah predicts the Assyrian invasion into Judah. Despite having an undefeated record in world conquest,[5] Assyria will attempt to siege Judah but will not prevail. Their defeat will not be due to human hands. Fulfilled during the reign of Assyrian King Sennacherib in approximately 701 BC.

TTF = 40 years (toward the end of Isaiah's life)

Fig. 5.4: Assyria's failed invasion of Judah

Historical Context

Assyria at the height of its empire had become the most powerful civilization the world had ever known. Under King Sennacherib the

Assyrians led an active campaign conquering most of the then world from Babylon, Moab, and Phoenicia all the way to Egypt.

The arrogance of this world dictator is hardly missed during an exchange with the leaders of Judah, in which his message is clear; pay higher taxes to the king of Assyria, or else be sacked. The messengers of Sennacherib readily taunt the people of Judah, claiming they will eat their own dung, drink their own urine, and be captured. His pretentious tone and mockery of Judah's hopelessness is so great that, in his estimation, providing their cavalry with supplies will make no difference in the outcome of such an encounter.

> "I will give you two thousand horses—if you can put riders on them!" (Isa 36:8).

In this predicament, Hezekiah calls for counsel from Isaiah, who gives a rather unexpected message:

> Devise your strategy, but it will be thwarted;
> propose your plan, but it will not stand,
> for God is with us. (Isa 8:10 NIV)
>
> I will defend this city and save it,
> for my sake and for the sake of David my servant!
> (Isa 37:35 NIV)

This is precisely what happened: the Assyrians experienced complications in capturing Jerusalem, and when Sennacherib saw the destruction wreaked on his army, he withdrew to Nineveh; Jerusalem was spared destruction.[6]

The Hebrew Bible states that during the night, an angel of Yahweh brought death to 185,000 Assyrians troops (2 Kings 19:35; Isa 37:36).

The Assyrian record on the matter is awfully silent; though under besiegement, Jerusalem is the only city during Sennacherib's reign of which capture is not mentioned.[7] History is somewhat ambiguous as to how the transfer of power occurred (whether by nature or assassination).

Nonetheless, following this event Sennacherib quickly died and was succeeded by Esarhaddon.

In other accounts, a water-borne disease such as cholera has become the leading explanation of the unexplainable withdrawal and death of Assyrian troops.[8]

Even still, Isaiah's prediction that the Assyrian defeat would not take place by human hands came true!

[Further readings: Isaiah 8; 31:8–9; 32–33; 37.]

3) The End of the Assyrian Empire

In addition to predicting a failed attempt at conquering Jerusalem, Isaiah repeatedly predicts the collapse of the Assyrian empire through various prophecies during the reigns of Ahaz and Hezekiah. Fulfilled in 612 BC during the Battle of Nineveh.

TTF = 104 years

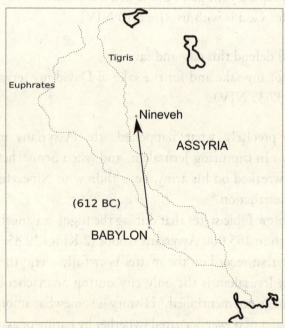

Fig. 5.5: Babylonian Invasion of Assyria

Historical Context

> Assyria's sudden collapse is so startling and unexpected as properly to cause surprise and demand investigation.[9]
> — George Stephen Goodspeed
> (*A History of the Babylonians and Assyrians*)

This mighty nation ruling for 700 years was virtually unchallenged, enjoying world dominance for the greater part of a millennium. In such a scenario Isaiah announces that the days of Assyria's kingdom are numbered, informing the kings of Judah of this nation's eventual fate. According to Isaiah's counsel, their pomp and arrogance were now beginning to challenge the God of Israel, and not only would they lose in Jerusalem (as previously noted), but their empire would meet its sudden demise.

Previously (during the reign of Ahaz), Isaiah portrayed Assyria as God's tool used for disciplining Israel (Northern Kingdom) and the surrounding nations. Yet at this point they have overstepped their bounds, challenging the God of Israel and as a result will be plundered by God himself, "Does the axe lift itself above the person who swings it?" (Isa 10:15 NIV; see vs. 5–34)

Furthermore, following the death of Ahaz, Isaiah twice mentions the eventual fate of the Assyrian nation. The first time is in chapter 14 (during a series of prophecies involving the Babylonians), where Isaiah predicts their involvement in the demise of Assyria (Isa 14:24–28).

Second, in chapter 30 he reiterates that Assyria will be beaten down through the voice of the Lord (Isaiah 30:27–33).

These predictions were ultimately fulfilled 110 years after Isaiah's decree;, culminating in the Battle of Nineveh, where a confederation of allies from Media, Persia, and Babylonia would join and sack Nineveh.[10] The demise of Assyria occurred quite rapidly followed by the rise of the world's next superpower, Babylon.

[Further readings: Isaiah 10; 14:24–27; 30.]

4) The Rise of Babylon as a New World Power

When Isaiah was writing, Babylon was an insignificant nation under the sway of mighty Assyria. Isaiah predicted the rise of Babylon as a newly emerging world power. This was fulfilled in 605 BC during the Battle of Carchemish,[11] when the allied armies of Egypt and former Assyria were defeated by the Babylonians for control of the Fertile Crescent.

TTF = 111 years

Historical Context

Isaiah, though deceased by this time (according to rabbinical texts, martyred by Manasseh in a tree trunk and sliced in half),[2] continues to live on through his writings; particularly in his comments on the fate of Babylon, which began to emerge as a powerful nation in 605 BC.

Foremost, inherent in the prophecies of chapters 13 and 14 are assumptions on Babylon's position in world affairs.

> And Babylon, the glory of kingdoms,
> The beauty of the Chaldeans' pride. (Isa 13:19)

> Your pomp is brought down to Sheol,
> And the sound of your stringed instruments. (Isa 14:11)

These prophecies are somewhat complex because they shift in scope from present day to the distant future, coupling the national Babylon in Isaiah's day with the "spiritual Babylon" alluded to in other writings of scripture. I refrain from entering into a deeper analysis on the nature of Babylon at this point. Nonetheless, what is clear in these passages is the assumption that the kingdom had reached a position of pomp, arrogance, and power among the nations at a time when their position in world affairs was rather obscure.

Other references found throughout Isaiah's text also imply Babylon's status as he predicts judgment against this nation.

[Further readings: Isaiah 13–14; 21:9; 39; 43:14; 48:14.]

5) Babylonian Captivity of the Jews

In addition to Babylon's rise to power, Isaiah predicts that the Babylonians will capture the wealth of Judah and many of its inhabitants. For instance, the items Hezekiah exhibited to the Babylonian messengers will be taken. Fulfilled in 597 BC and 586 BC; Babylon takes captives and sacks Jerusalem the first time, then totally destroys Jerusalem about ten years later. This is the beginning of what is known as the *Babylonian Exile*.

TTF = 130 years

In chapter 39, we have the narrative of Hezekiah's sickness during which visitors coming from Babylon arrive with gifts and condolences for the king of Judah. Flattered by their generosity, Hezekiah decides to show these visitors all the treasuries of his kingdom. Isaiah, arriving at the scene rather late, informs Hezekiah that he has just made a terrible mistake. He predicts that these items will be carried off to Babylon together with captives from the land of Judah.

> Then Isaiah said to Hezekiah, "Hear the word of the Lord Almighty: The time will surely come when everything in your palace, and all that your predecessors have stored up until this day, will be carried off to Babylon. Nothing will be left, says the Lord. And some of your descendants, your own flesh and blood who will be born to you, will be taken away, and they will become eunuchs in the palace of the king of Babylon." (Isa 39:5–7 NIV)

[Further readings: Isaiah 39.]

6) Babylon's Demise

After its rise to power, Isaiah predicts the fall of Babylon, identifying the nation to perform it, even the name of the leader who will lead the charge. Fulfilled in 539 BC during the Medo-Persian invasions.[12]

TTF = 177 years

Historical Context

Babylon, at its height, was one of the glories of the ancient world; its walls and mythic hanging gardens are listed among the Seven Wonders of the World.[13] Its demise would be difficult to conceive of, not only during the time of Isaiah, but even centuries afterward when the Babylonian Empire became fully established.

Yet during the reigns of Ahaz and Hezekiah, Isaiah makes a couple of related predictions pertaining to the downward fate of Babylon. His claim is that, just as Sodom and Gomorrah were destroyed, Babylon would be as well.

> And Babylon, the glory of kingdoms,
> The beauty of the Chaldeans' pride,
> Will be as when God overthrew Sodom and Gomorrah.
> It will never be inhabited,
> Nor will it be settled from generation to generation;
> Nor will the Arabian pitch tents there,
> Nor will the shepherds make their sheepfolds there. (Isa 13:19–20)

This was fulfilled in 539 BC when the Medo-Persians took Babylon.[15]

[Further readings: Isaiah 13; 20; 44.]

7) The Establishment of the Medo-Persian Alliance

Isaiah predicts the establishment of the Medo-Persian alliance that will ultimately defeat the mighty nation of Babylon. Fulfilled in 549 BC when Cyrus and the Persians conquered the Medes to form a powerful alliance.[12]

TTF = 202 years / 465 years

Historical Context

As we have seen previously, Isaiah not only predicts the downfall of Babylon but also foresees the alliance that will form to bring about their demise as seen in the phrase: "Elam, attack! Media, lay siege!" (Isaiah 21:2 NIV). These nations working together will facilitate the collapse of this mighty world power.

Interestingly enough, Isaiah uses the label *Elam* instead of *Persia*. The Elamites were an ethnic subgroup who later assimilated into the Persian empire.[14]

> A dire vision has been shown to me:
> The traitor betrays, the looter takes loot.
> Elam, attack! Media, lay siege!
> I will bring to an end all the groaning she caused. (Isa 21:2 NIV)
>
> Look, here comes a man in a chariot
> with a team of horses.
> And he gives back the answer:
> "Babylon has fallen, has fallen!
> All the images of its gods
> lie shattered on the ground!" (Isa 21:9 NIV)
>
> Behold, I will stir up the Medes against them,
> Who will not regard silver;
> And as for gold, they will not delight in it. (Isa 13:17)

Historical documents on the Persians and Elamites are somewhat obscure. However, records indicate that by 522–486 BC, Elam was fully absorbed into the Persian Empire, and from that point on the two nations were virtually indistinguishable.[14] Also of note, the name *Cyrus*—the great leader who led the military campaign of these allied nations—is believed to have Elamite etymological roots.

[Further readings: Isa 13:17–18; 21.]

8) Cyrus the Great Predicted

Isaiah identifies the name of the Medo-Persian leader who will rise to defeat the Babylonians and lead the emancipation of the Hebrews from captivity. Fulfilled in 539 BC during the Medo-Persian invasion where, according to sources, water from the Euphrates River was diverted, allowing forces to enter the city at night.[15]

TTF = 201 years

Historical Context

Further adding to the specificities of Isaiah's prophecies on the fall of Babylon, he not only mentions the unlikely fall of the world's greatest empire to date (foreseeing the political alliances that will perform it) but also specifies the name of the world leader who will arise and lead these armies.

Cyrus, born in Persia to parents of both Persian (father) and Median descent (mother), used his family background to unify the Medes and the Persians, even gaining legitimacy as ruler in both kingdoms alike.[12]

Following his conquest of Babylon, he allowed the captive Israelites to return back home, essentially ending the Babylonian Captivity.[16] This was predicted centuries before in Isaiah 44 and 45.

> Who says of Cyrus, 'He is My shepherd,
> And he shall perform all My pleasure,
> Saying to Jerusalem, "You shall be built,"

And to the temple, "Your foundation shall be laid."'
(Isa 44:28)

"Thus says the Lord to His anointed,
To Cyrus, whose right hand I have held—
To subdue nations before him
And loose the armor of kings,
To open before him the double doors,
So that the gates will not be shut: ...
For Jacob My servant's sake,
And Israel My elect,
I have even called you by your name;
I have named you, though you have not known Me.
(Isa 45:1, 4)

As predicted, Cyrus was not a Jew and did not know the God of Jacob, yet he was instrumental in liberating the nation of Israel—God's chosen nation. In *Antiquities of the Jews,* the historian Josephus also mentions that Cyrus was shown the Isaiah scroll after his ascension to power.[16]

[Further readings: Isaiah 44–45.]

9) The Establishment of Five Jewish Cities in Egypt, One by the Name of Heliopolis

In a series of prophecies directed toward Egypt, Isaiah includes the prediction that five cities in Egypt will speak the Hebrew language; one of these cities will be named "City of the Sun."

This was fulfilled during the Ptolemaic era of 305 BC–30 BC, following the conquest of Alexander the Great in Egypt. Under their rule, the Greeks permitted the establishment of Jewish quarters within these Egyptian cities.[17] One of the cities was called *Heliopolis,* which means "City of the Sun."[18]

TTF = 716 - 250 = 466 years

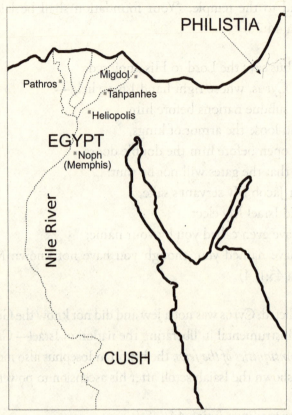

Fig. 5.6: Egyptian cities with Jewish Quarters

Historical Context

In that day five cities in Egypt will speak the language of Canaan and swear allegiance to the LORD Almighty. One of them will be called the City of the Sun. (Isa 19:18 NIV)

This was fulfilled in 331 BC when Alexander the Great easily conquered the land of Egypt. His reputation as a world leader was slightly different than that of previous dynasties such as the Babylonians or Assyrians, who subjected the conquered to cruel and humiliating subordination. Rather, Alexander allowed for the continuation of national and religious life so long as the appropriate patronage (usually in the form of taxes) was given to Alexander.[19]

It is in this environment that several Jewish communities began to flourish in Egypt. According to historical records, the cities with thriving Jewish communities occurred at Tahpanhes, Noph, Migdol, Pathros, and Heliopolis.[20]

In fact, sources have it that during the Ptolemaic rule, the Jews controlled their own districts in order to observe Mosaic Laws alongside Egyptian and Greek citizens now in the region. Thus, previously most Jews were coerced into Egypt as slaves; now many of them migrated willingly in light of these flourishing Jewish communities.[21]

Coincidentally, it is also during this era when the Old Testament was translated from Hebrew to Greek in the Septuagint (LXX). The Egyptians funded 72 scholars to accomplish this task, which turned out to be the main translation during the continued growth and influence of the Greek culture, a translation eventually used by Jesus and the early disciples a few centuries later.[22]

[Further readings: Isaiah 19:18.]

10) An Altar to the God of Israel Built in the Middle of Egypt

Besides the large population of Jews in Egyptian cities, Isaiah also predicts the establishment of Jewish worship centers in Egypt. This was fulfilled during multiple events beginning in 150 BC when Onias, an exiled priest from Judah, received the approval of Cleopatra to rebuild a temple in Heliopolis.

TTF = 566

Historical Context

The Hellenization of Egypt was, generally speaking, advantageous to the Jewish nation.

The allotment of land to Jews in Egypt, wherein the community of Hebrews represented here could freely observe kosher laws and perform other religious practices, offered the descendents of Abraham treatment as nothing less than first-class citizens in this nation. This is readily observed in the establishment of Jewish worship centers, a commodity not offered elsewhere in the history of Jewish captivity.

Accordingly, Isaiah had predicted this Egyptian favor centuries before in chapter 19, making the claim that worship of the Hebrew God would occur in the heart of Egypt: "In that day there will be an altar to the Lord in the heart of Egypt, and a monument to the Lord at its border" (Isa 19:19 NIV).

A wide array of historical accounts have been unearthed supporting the fulfillment of this passage. For instance, below is an excerpt of a letter where Cleopatra gives approval for the erection of a Jewish temple. Onias, the priest from Judah who submits the request, cites Isaiah 19 as part of his justifications for needing the temple:

> We have read thy petition, wherein thou desirest leave to be given thee to purge that temple which is fallen down at Leontopolis, in the Nome of Heliopolis, and which is named from the country Bubastis; on which account we cannot but wonder that it should be pleasing to God to have a temple erected in a place so unclean, and so full of sacred animals. But since thou sayest that Isaiah the prophet foretold this long ago, we give thee leave to do it, if it may be done according to your law, and so that we may not appear to have at all offended God herein.[23]

Furthermore, the writings of Josephus provide additional records of this event: "Onias found other Jews like to himself, together with priests and Levites, that there performed Divine service. But we have said enough about this temple."[24]

Additional historical accounts supporting this fulfillment were also discovered by Egyptian farmers in the archive of Ananiah and Tamut on Elephantine Island in 1893. The Elephantine Papyri also makes mention of a second temple being erected.[25]

[*Further readings: Isaiah 19:19.*]

Conclusion

As we bring the prophecies in Bucket A to a close, it should be stated that this grouping of prophecies for this era is by no means exhaustive. For instance, the following predictions (which can be an exercise to the reader) have been omitted: (11) The Desolation of Tyre, (12) The Defeat of the Moabites (which causes Isaiah to weep), and (13) An Egyptian Civil War.

IDENTIFYING THE LORD'S SERVANT

CHAPTER SIX

Will the real servant please stand up?

While the prophecies in Bucket A were fulfilled over a span of 1000 years, the prophecies in Bucket B are mostly fulfilled during a brief period of time surrounding a single character, "God's Servant." However, before proceeding with these prophecies, it seems necessary to take a brief detour in setting up the context for the following predictions.

As was mentioned in chapter 1, in chapters 40–53 we repeatedly encounter a somewhat ambiguous phrase ("My Servant," "the Servant of Yahweh," etc.) used a total of fifteen times.

Below is a list of such references from this section:

Reference	Excerpt	Portrayal
Isa 41:8-9	"But you, Israel, My servant, Jacob whom I have chosen, Descendant of Abraham My friend … 'You are My servant, I have chosen you and not rejected you."	Negative
Isa 42:1	"Behold, My Servant, whom I uphold; My chosen one [in whom] My soul delights …"	Positive
Isa 42:19	"Who is blind but My servant, Or so deaf as My messenger whom I send? Who is so blind as he that is at peace [with Me,] Or so blind as the servant of the LORD"	Negative
Isa 43:10	"'You are My witnesses,' declares the LORD, 'And My servant whom I have chosen, So that you may know and believe Me And understand that I am He.' … "	Negative
Isa 44:1	"But now listen, O Jacob, My servant, And Israel, whom I have chosen …"	Negative
Isa 44:21	"Remember these things, O Jacob, And Israel, for you are My servant; I have formed you, you are My servant, O Israel, you will not be forgotten by Me.'…"	Negative
Isa 45:4	"For the sake of Jacob My servant, And Israel My chosen [one,] I have also called you by your name; I have given you a title of honor Though you have not known Me."	Negative
Isa 48:20	o forth from Babylon! Flee from the Chaldeans! Declare with the sound of joyful shouting, proclaim this, Send it out to the end of the earth; Say, "The LORD has redeemed His servant Jacob."	Negative
Isa 49:3-6	"You are My Servant, Israel, In Whom I will show My glory." … "And now says the LORD, who formed Me from the womb to be His Servant, To bring Jacob back to Him, so that Israel might be gathered to Him" … He says, "It is too small a thing that You should be My Servant To raise up the tribes of Jacob and to restore the preserved ones of Israel; I will also make You a light of the nations So that My salvation may reach to the end of the earth."	Positive
Isa 50:10	"Who is among you that fears the LORD, That obeys the voice of His servant …"	Positive
Isa 52:13	"Behold, My servant will prosper, He will be high and lifted up and greatly exalted"	Positive
Isa 53:11	"… By His knowledge the Righteous One, My Servant, will justify the many, As He will bear their iniquities."	Positive

*References from NASB

Fig 6.1: Uses of the word "Servant" from Ch. 40–53

There has been much debate on the identity of said individual. Who is this servant? Isaiah, Cyrus, Hezekiah, or perhaps some other notable figure? Still others have taken this word to be a symbol for the nation of Israel, a collective personification of the chosen people.

In order to better answer this question, we will need to examine these passages more closely.

Positive and Negative Contrasts

First, as you read through this section, observe the contrasting descriptions (favorable vs. unfavorable) given in each mention of "My Servant." Here's an example from chapter 42 illustrating this distinction:

> Behold! My Servant whom I uphold,
> My Elect One in whom My soul delights!
> I have put My Spirit upon Him;
> He will bring forth justice to the Gentiles. (Isa 42:1)

> Who is blind but my servant,
> and deaf like the messenger I send?
> Who is blind like the one in covenant with me,
> blind like the servant of the Lord? ...
> Who gave up Jacob to the looter,
> and Israel to the plunderers?
> Was it not the Lord, against whom we have sinned,
> in whose ways they would not walk,
> and whose law they would not obey? (Isa 42:19 NIV; 42:24 ESV)

In the first reference above, Isaiah highlights the wisdom and obedience of the servant, who is a "delight" to the Lord. Yet In the second reference, we are told, to the contrary, that this servant is stubborn, disobedient, even "deaf and blind." Are both of these references referring to the same person or entity?

This mixture of portrayals occurs repeatedly throughout this section; in about half of the references the servant is shown in an extremely positive light, and in the other half the servant is an utter failure, sinful, and useless. How then, can this disparity be reconciled?

The Shifting of Writing Styles: Poetry, Narrative

As we examine the text more closely, it turns out that in the positive portrayals of "My Servant," the text breaks from its typical narrative prose, and the references are contained in what appear to be poems or songs (a pattern better observed in the original Hebrew text).[1]

These passages are famously known as the Servant Songs:[2]

1. Isaiah 42:1–4
2. Isaiah 49:1–6
3. Isaiah 50:4–9
4. Isaiah 52:13–53:12

Given this shift in writing style, it seems as if he is making a prominent distinction in these sections, providing a comparison between two different servants. What other clues do we have in deciphering this conundrum?

An Individual, Not a Group

First-Person Address

Another consideration here is that in two of the *Servant Songs* (Isa. 49:1–6; 50:4–9), there is a noted grammatical difference when referring to "the Servant," namely, the use of the first person: in these passages the Servant is the speaker. Observe how in the following passage, the Servant (speaker) refers to both Jacob and Israel—the collective nation—as a different entity.

> Then I said, 'I have labored in vain,
> I have spent my strength for nothing and in vain;

> Yet surely my just reward is with the Lord,
> And my work with my God.'
> And now the Lord says,
> Who formed <u>Me</u> from the womb to be <u>His Servant</u>,
> To bring <u>Jacob</u> back to Him,
> So that <u>Israel</u> is gathered to Him (Isa 49:4-5)

This begins to challenge the interpretation that *all of these* instances are symbolic for the collective nation.

Mission

Moreover, it should also be noticed how the assignment (or activity) of this servant appears to be directed toward the entire nation of Israel, collectively.

Below are some examples demonstrating both of these variances:

> For He was cut off from the land of the living;
> For the transgressions of My people He was stricken. (Isa 53:8)

> Surely he has borne our griefs and carried our sorrows; yet we esteemed him stricken, smitten by God, and afflicted. (Isa 53:4 ESV)

> Out of the anguish of his soul he shall see and be satisfied; by his knowledge shall the righteous *one*, my servant, make many to be accounted righteous, and he shall bear their iniquities. (Isa 53:11 ESV, emphasis added)

In considering these passages, how then, can the collective nation be used to gather the nation itself? How can my people suffer for my people? If we take the Servant in this case to be the entire nation of Israel—all of the Jews in a collective personality—the passage fails to mean anything; Isaiah must be talking about one individual in *some* of these cases.

Unknown Identities: **Missing a reference to the name *Jacob***

Finally, we consider another oddity found in the Servant Songs. Not only is there a difference in writing style in these positive portrayals of the servant, but the usual identifying reference (Jacob and Israel) is missing. In every other passage where the Servant is given an explicit identity to be the entire Jewish nation, the paired address to Jacob and Israel is included. Yet surprisingly, whenever the servant is spoken of in a positive light, the reference to Jacob is missing, or no reference is provided at all! (We find no such reference in three of these four Servant Songs.)

Here are some examples of this paired address:

> But you, Israel, my servant,
> Jacob, whom I have chosen,
> the offspring of Abraham, my friend. (Isa 41:8 ESV)

> Listen to me, Jacob,
> Israel, whom I have called. (Isa 48:12 NIV)

And here some examples without the paired address:

> Behold, my servant shall act wisely;
> he shall be high and lifted up,
> and shall be exalted. (Isa 52:13 ESV)

> Behold my servant, whom I uphold,
> my chosen, in whom my soul delights;
> I have put my Spirit upon him;
> he will bring forth justice to the nations. (Isa 42:1 ESV)

Reference to Jacob removed:

> He said to me, "You are my servant,
> Israel, in whom I will display my splendor." (Isa 49:3 NIV)

I believe this to be the key to deciphering this enigma. It's as if when the reference to Jacob is included, he is speaking to the nation—which was intended to be God's servant but failed. When this reference is omitted, he is speaking of a future servant, an individual who will successfully carry out God's task, even benefiting the failed servant.

Notice below the passages that contain an explicit reference, occurring a total of 18 times in this section:

1. Isa 40:27	7. Isa 43:28	13. Isa 45:4
2. Isa 41:8	8. Isa 44:1	14. Isa 46:3
3. Isa 41:14	9. Isa 44:2 *Jeshurun	15. Isa 48:1
4. Isa 42:24	10. Isa 44:5	16. Isa 48:12
5. Isa 43:1	11. Isa 44:21	17. Isa 49:5
6. Isa 43:22	12. Isa 44:23	18. Isa 49:6

Fig. 6.2: References to Jacob and Israel from Ch. 40–53

The Implication of Jacob

So what is significant about the omission of Jacob?

Recall that the nation of Israel was initially called Jacob (Ya'akov), but when he attempted to steal the birthright, God permanently changed his name to Israel: "You shall no longer be called Jacob, But Israel shall be your name" (Genesis 35:10).

Thus, in *Jacob* we have the old name, which incidentally means "deceiver" or "supplanter,"[4] a remembrance of the failed nation that did not succeed in accomplishing God's mission. Yet in *Israel* we have a new name, a glorious future, and a reminder of God's continued covenant promise with his people.

This usage of contrasting Jacob with Israel is mentioned by Rabbi Samson Raphael Hirsch in his commentary on Genesis: "The name Jacob, he maintains, connects with the stooped, downcast man whereas the name Israel connotes hope and reinvigoration."[5]

Conclusion

In considering the context of this section, I believe the answer will be abundantly clear. Recall that in this section, Isaiah's aim is to offer the rebellious nation words of comfort in their moment of exile. He does so in cycles, which increase in intensity, as he approaches a climax in chapter 53. His message is that their sins will be forgiven and their rebellious ways pardoned; that these idols and nations (which have subdued Israel) will be crushed.

By interpreting these uses of "My Servant" as contrasts between two different entities—a failed nation in exile as opposed to a successful servant who is wise and obedient (Jacob vs. Israel)—Isaiah's message of comfort becomes apparent. The successful mission of God's servant (the faithful one), is motive for hope and comfort toward God's servant (the disobedient one). Though currently in exile, she will be redeemed by the faithful one; a different kind of servant whose character is impeccable.

As we explore the predictions in Bucket B, the hope is that the identity of this servant will become even more evident and that the "the Arm of the Lord" will be revealed, personally. As we examine these predictions, it will be difficult not to think of one particular Jew—one who, according to the Gospels, would faithfully carry out God's will, even to the point of death: Y'shua, the Son of David.

BUCKET B: MESSIANIC PREDICTIONS

CHAPTER SEVEN

1) The Dreadful Murder of the Lord's Servant

Included in Isaiah's discourse on the "Servant of the Lord," he predicts that the well-instructed, wise, and obedient servant will undergo a tragic and humiliating death. This is paralleled in the New Testament with the crucifixion of Jesus; a servant who is similarly portrayed as wise and innocent, who also experiences an unjust death.

TTF = 750 years (AD 30–33)

Historical Context

As mentioned previously, one of the main focuses of the section of Isaiah from chapters 42 through 53 is the character referred to as the "Servant of the Lord." The tragedy here is that though he is described in such high esteem, he will be rejected by his own people and murdered in a horrifically unjust way.

In chapters 52–53, corresponding to the fourth *Servant Song*, we are told that this individual is beaten so intensely that he is no longer recognizable as a human.

> Just as there were many who were appalled at him—
> his appearance was so disfigured beyond that of any human being

and his form marred beyond human likeness— (Isa 52:14 NIV)

The crucifixion of Jesus as portrayed in the Gospels is a fulfillment of this passage, where one referred to as a servant with wise teachings and of humble character is castigated to the point of death, even rejected by his own people and closest friends.

According to biblical scholar Christopher M. Tucket, the crucifixion of Jesus is one of the most indisputable facts of history.[1]

The apostle Paul makes this connection supremely—linking Isaiah's servant to Jesus Christ—in his letter to the Philippians. He tells us of a servant who, though humiliated to the point of death, will be highly exalted. (We will say more about this passage's connection to Isaiah in chapter 11, *New Testament Allusions*.)

> He made himself nothing
> by taking the very nature of a servant,
> being made in human likeness.
> And being found in appearance as a man,
> he humbled himself
> by becoming obedient to death—
> even death on a cross!
> Therefore God exalted him to the highest place
> and gave him the name that is above every name.
> (Philippians 2:7–9 NIV)

[Further readings: Isaiah 50; 52; 53.]

2) A Submissive Servant Who Does Not Fight Back

Continuing further in his predictions on the Suffering Servant, we learn that during the assassination of this highly esteemed servant, he will not fight back, even while enduring spittings, mockings, and scourgings but will instead remain submissive to the process.

TTF = 750 years

Historical Context

As mentioned previously, Isaiah tells us that the Servant will be submissive during his execution, though he is castigated severely, he does not fight back and will comply with the procedure. Most criminals undergoing crucifixion would typically retaliate with words and resistance;[2] yet, the Servant of the Lord does not. He remains silent.

> I offered my back to those who beat me,
> my cheeks to those who pulled out my beard;
> I did not hide my face
> from mocking and spitting. (Isa 50:6 NIV)

> He was oppressed and afflicted,
> yet he did not open his mouth;
> he was led like a lamb to the slaughter,
> and as a sheep before its shearers is silent,
> so he did not open his mouth. (Isa 53:7 NIV)

This was also true of Jesus during his execution. Below is a description from Mark's gospel:

> The high priest stood up and came forward and questioned Jesus, saying, "Do You not answer? What is it that these men are testifying against You?" But He kept silent and did not answer. Again the high priest was questioning Him, and saying to Him, "Are You the Christ, the Son of the Blessed One?" (Mark 14:60–61 NASB)

[Further readings: Isaiah 50:6; 53; Matthew 26:67; Mark 15; Luke 23:9.]

3) Widespread Acceptance beyond the Jewish Nation

Isaiah makes repeated predictions that other nations (even distant islands) will put their hope in the teachings of this Servant. This was fulfilled initially on the day of Pentecost (*Shavuot*), when the teachings of Jesus—though originating from a Jewish subculture—began to spread to other nations and ethnic groups, a movement that continues even to the present day.

TTF = 750 years

Historical Context

Historically, worship of the Jewish God was restricted to those of Jewish descent.[3] However, in various portions of Isaiah's prophecies he predicts the spreading of the Jewish religion to non-Jews, extending to foreigners and eunuchs. In his depictions of the wise servant, he repeatedly claims that the teachings of the wise servant will be accepted by other nations, even becoming a light to the Gentiles.

> I will also make you a light for the Gentiles,
>   that my salvation may reach to the ends of the earth.
> (Isa 49:6 NIV)

> He will not falter or be discouraged
>   till he establishes justice on earth.
> In his teaching the islands will put their hope. (Isa 42:4 NIV)

This became true of the ministry of Jesus starting on the day of Pentecost. A humble servant who was brutally beaten, his teachings have reached virtually every continent and people group. This is quite remarkable, considering that he never wrote anything during his three short years of active ministry.

[Further readings: Isaiah 42:6; 49:6; 52:10; 60:3; John 8:12.]

4) Rejected by Many, Acquainted with Sorrows

Isaiah predicts that during the execution of the Servant, he will be rejected and despised by men. Likewise, during the crucifixion of Jesus, everyone turned their backs on him—even his own friends and closest disciples.

TTF = 750 years

Historical Context

In the accounts of Jesus's crucifixion, the Gospels make it clear that he was physically tortured. Yet perhaps the greatest pain he experienced was not physical but rather the pain of emotional abandonment: he was rejected even by those closest to him.

Pontius Pilate, convicted by the seemingly upright character of Jesus and unsure of his criminal status, decided to let the crowds make the final determination of his fate by allowing one of the prisoners up for crucifixion to be released. The crowds chose Barabbas (a rebel against Roman power[4])—the same crowds that only a few days earlier were exuberant at his appearance, shouting, "Hosanna! Blessed is he who comes in the name of the Lord." Others close to him asked questions like, "Can anything good come from Nazareth?" "Isn't this just the carpenter's son?" Even his biological half-brother, James, would be unbelieving until the moment of his resurrection.

Adding further to his despair was the rejection by his closest friends—even Peter, who, earlier on the day of his crucifixion, had promised he would never do such a thing.

> He was despised and rejected by mankind,
> a man of suffering, and familiar with pain. (Isa 53:3 NIV)

Nonetheless, the greatest pain he must have experienced was when the Father turned his back on Jesus as he was bearing the sins of humanity.

And about the ninth hour Jesus cried out with a loud voice, saying, "Eli, Eli, lama sabachthani?" that is, "My God, My God, why have You forsaken Me?" (Matthew 27:46)

[Further readings: Isaiah 53:6.]

5) His Death Will Serve as Atonement for Sins

The death of the Servant will serve as atonement for "my people." This was fulfilled in the crucifixion of Jesus where, according to the scriptures, his death became the propitiation for the sins of humanity.

TTF = 750 years

Historical Context

In the account of the Suffering Servant's death, Isaiah interestingly remarks that he will suffer for the sins of "my people," thus providing the necessary atonement, as was common throughout the Old Testament, through the use of animals; his anguish would become a source of healing and salvation to others.

According to the New Testament writers, this was one of the reasons for the death of Jesus. The writer of Hebrews compares the blood of Jesus at the cross to that of animals used in atoning services.

> He did not enter by means of the blood of goats and calves; but he entered the Most Holy Place once for all by his own blood, thus obtaining eternal redemption. (Hebrews 9:12 NIV)

> But he was pierced for our transgressions,
> he was crushed for our iniquities. (Isa 53:5 NIV)

[Further readings: Isaiah 53.]

6) Buried with the Rich

In the fourth Servant Song (Isaiah 52–53), where the death of the suffering servant is explored in greater detail, Isaiah makes the remark that though this servant would be crucified with the wicked, he would be buried with the rich. Consider how unusual this statement would be in light of the rejection and betrayal Isaiah claims he will experience. Who would give such an individual a proper burial? Or even still, with the rich?

This prediction was astonishingly fulfilled during the burial of Jesus. In what is a somewhat embarrassing fact about the life of Jesus: neither his closest friends nor his family members took the initiative to provide a proper burial. History tells us of a man by the name of Joseph of Arimathea. As a wealthy member of the Sanhedrin (governmental religious council)—which conducted the trial and sentencing of Jesus—Joseph took it upon himself to give Jesus a proper burial, fulfilling the aforementioned remarks of Isaiah.[5]

[Further readings: Isaiah 53:9.]

7) Resurrection of the Servant

In addition to predicting that the Suffering Servant would be rejected by men and buried with the rich, Isaiah also makes this most striking prediction as well; he claims that even though he has perished, he will see the light of life and witness his offspring again.

TTF = 750 years

Historical Context

According to New Testament scholar, N. T. Wright, the concept of resurrection from the dead was practically nonexistent in the ancient Jewish world.[6]

Yet, Isaiah still writes that one who is beaten to death will see the "light of life." Isaiah's contemporaries must have pondered how this dead servant would have his days prolonged and, as was mentioned at the beginning of the stanza, how he would reach the top, even becoming highly exalted.

> He will see his offspring and prolong his days,
> and the will of the LORD will prosper in his hand.
> After he has suffered,
> he will see the light of life and be satisfied. (Isa 53:10 NIV)

This seemingly preposterous prediction details one of the main tenets about Jesus espoused in the New Testament, namely his resurrection from the dead.

His resurrection became a central teaching of those who ended up following him. In fact, according to Paul in 1 Corinthians 15:17 (ESV), "If Christ has not been raised, your faith is futile and you are still in your sins."

Much has been written on the historical grounds for belief in the resurrection of Jesus. For further reading, consult works such as William Lane Craig's *The Resurrection of Jesus* or N. T. Wright's *The Resurrection of the Son of God*.

[Further readings: Isaiah 53:11.]

BUCKET C: ESCHATOLOGICAL PREDICTIONS

CHAPTER EIGHT

Isaiah's panoramic perspective from 700 BC includes predictions on world events that have yet to occur.

The futuristic accounts offered here are very much consistent with other eschatological texts in both the Old Testament (Psalms, Daniel, Ezekiel, Zechariah, etc.) and the New Testament (the Gospels, 2 Thessalonians, Revelation, etc.). Cross-examination of these texts is greatly encouraged as it reveals the grand picture of biblical harmony. Though penned by a myriad of independent writers spanning a wide range of time, the monumental biblical axioms are presented with magnificent consistency.

If Isaiah was correct concerning his predictions in Buckets A and B, how much more relevant the study of his predictions on future days should be.

1a) Multinational Worship of the Jewish God in Mount Zion

Isaiah predicts that "In the Latter Days," people of all nations will go up to Mount Zion and worship the Jewish God. According to Isaiah's vision from chapter 2, the multiethnic sounds of worship will include representation from all people groups—even the distant islands.

Moreover, this prophetic glimpse of multinational worship is also mentioned in chapters 24–27, where Isaiah hears songs of praise, "Glory to the righteous one," coming from the coastlands even to the ends of the earth. These predictions, envisioning the "Latter Days," occur in juxtaposition to the destruction of the earth and the global judgment of wickedness.

[Further readings: Isaiah 2, 24–27.]

1b) The Triple Alliance of Egypt, Assyria, and Judah

As an extension of the previous prediction (global worship of the Jewish god), Isaiah is sure to mention a particular three-part alliance between Egypt, Assyria, and Judah. Though in his present day, these nations were not on favorable terms, he specifically mentions that even these three will join together to worship the Jewish God and will be a blessing to the earth.

[Further readings: Isaiah 19:24–25; 27:13.]

2) World Peace

The judgments of the God of Jacob will serve to usher in world peace and global harmony, even extending into nature and the animal kingdom.

> "The wolf and the lamb will feed together, and the lion will eat straw like the ox, and dust will be the serpent's food. They will neither harm nor destroy on all my holy mountain," says the LORD. (Isa 65:25 NIV)

> The wolf shall dwell with the lamb,
> and the leopard shall lie down with the young goat,
> and the calf and the lion and the fattened calf together;
> and a little child shall lead them. (Isa 11:6 ESV)

These effects are seen as direct results of the establishment of Messiah's kingdom and his judgments on the earth; the restoration of the paradise lost in the garden.

Accordingly, there will be an end to all wars; military equipment once used for warfare and destruction will be discarded or instead repurposed and used for farming as indicated in phrases such as "They shall beat their swords into plowshares" (Isaiah 2:4).

Many international peace groups have attempted (and still are) to bring this to fruition,[1] but Isaiah is clear in stating that the God of Jacob will be the party responsible for such an action: "He will judge between the nations and will settle disputes for many peoples" (Isaiah 2:4 NIV).

A similar concept is expressed in Isaiah 9, this time, however, attributed to a child with the government on his shoulders. (This concept will be explored in greater detail in chapter 10, *Eschatological Mix-Ups*.)

> Every warrior's boot used in battle
> and every garment rolled in blood
> will be destined for burning,
> will be fuel for the fire. (Isa 9:5 NIV)

[Further readings: Isaiah 2; 9; 11; 65.]

3) God's Anointed Messiah (*Mashiach* or Christ) Will Govern Perpetually

In a time of great turmoil and utter darkness in the nation of Israel, Isaiah offers comfort with the message that in the days ahead there is coming "a great light" in the form of a "child to be born."

This child is given the title of "Everlasting father" or "my father you are forever," something of a Hebrew prayer usually directed toward God himself. The government will be put on his shoulders and never be taken back. He will be eternity's unchallenged king and, according to the leadership of King David, will rule eternally, from Jerusalem, with justice and righteousness.

The same prediction is made in the book of Revelation where John states that "the kingdoms of this world have become the kingdoms of our Lord and of His Christ" (11:15). As the drama unfolds in Revelation, we learn that Jesus is predicted to rule perpetually, thus fulfilling the description of Isaiah 9. To readers in Isaiah's day, it must have seemed preposterous that a mere mortal—a child to be born—could take on the role of a perpetual father. How is this possible? This also supports one of the main tenets of the identity of Jesus, which we will explore in Part 3.

[Further readings: Isaiah 9; 16:5.]

4) The Destruction of Babylon

Isaiah's predictions concerning the present-day political state of Babylon are sometimes intertwined with the "spiritual Babylon." For instance, included in this prophecy—directed to Babylon and its king (chapter 14)—is a description of Lucifer and his fall from glory. Many of Isaiah's descriptions and decrees from this section simply do not fit the historical Babylon (circa 700 BC).

Among the group of prophecies concerning the "spiritual Babylon," Isaiah predicts that a multiethnic army will bring about the ultimate defeat of their political system: "Listen, an uproar among the kingdoms, like nations massing together!" (Isaiah 13:4 NIV).

Additionally, statements such as "See, the day of the LORD is coming" provide hints that this is referring to the day of recompense on the final day of judgment. Further support of this view comes from the similarities found in his description of their demise with that of the "Day of the Lord" or "that day" in other passages (such as Matthew 24 and Isaiah 24:23), as evidenced in details such as the sun and moon being darkened.

In many ways, the narrative of scriptures throughout the Bible revolves around these two cities: Babylon and Jerusalem. Spiritually, Babylon represents the "city of man," where the fundamental value is self-centeredness and a reliance on man's independence and achievement. This is demonstrated even in the book of Genesis at the tower of Babel:

> They said, "Come, let us build ourselves a city, and a tower whose top is in the heavens; let us make a name for ourselves, lest we be scattered abroad over the face of the whole earth." (Genesis 11:4)

On the other hand, Jerusalem——which incidentally means, "New Peace"—represents God's city and is founded on a different kind of value system. Here Yahweh is rightly acknowledged as the source of all—a dependence on him.

Isaiah predicts that the Babylonian system will be present up to the "Day of Judgment," when it will ultimately fall. Interestingly enough, the word *Babylon* appears in 1 Peter 5:13 but is applied to Rome; perhaps at the time they were being governed by a great Babylonic influence. In addition, according to Isaiah 47, Babylon is personified as a harlot who will eventually be brought low.

For a deeper understanding on the nature of Babylon, these predictions should be cross-compared with other mentions in the books of Daniel and Revelation.

[Further readings: Isaiah 13; 14; 47.]

5) The Destruction of Earth and the Creation of the New Heavens and New Earth

In the process of the universal judgment that will occur on the "Day of the Lord," Isaiah predicts that the earth will be destroyed and replaced with "New Heavens" and a "New Earth."

The judgments in chapter 24 can be contrasted with the restoration of paradise in chapter 65, where Jerusalem will be a delight forever.

> The earth will be completely laid waste
> and totally plundered.
> The LORD has spoken this word. (Isa 24:3 NIV)

> See, I will create
> new heavens and a new earth ....
> I will rejoice over Jerusalem
> and take delight in my people;
> the sound of weeping and of crying
> will be heard in it no more. (Isa 65:17, 19 NIV)

These predictions are related to God's global campaign of restoring the earth.

[Further readings: Isaiah 24; 66; 13:13.]

6) Brutal Extermination of Wickedness

In the process, the righteous will experience joy, but the wicked will suffer. The fury of the God of Jacob is so intense that the wicked will seek to hide in caves in order to escape the wrath that will be poured out.

> People will flee to caves in the rocks
> and to holes in the ground
> from the fearful presence of the LORD
> and the splendor of his majesty,
> when he rises to shake the earth. (Isa 2:19 NIV)

> In that day the Lord will punish
> the powers in the heavens above
> and the kings on the earth below. (Isa 24:21 NIV)

> Behold, My servants will shout joyfully with a glad heart,
> But you will cry out with a heavy heart,
> And you will wail with a broken spirit.
> You will leave your name for a curse to My chosen ones,
> And the Lord GOD will slay you. (Isa 65:14–15 NASB)

Consistent with how Isaiah views these events, other passages throughout scripture also attest to the twofold nature of the day of judgment; many times calling it "the great and terrible day," where the righteous rejoice and the wicked are fiercely annihilated. (Joel 2:11; Zephaniah 1:14; Malachi 4:5, etc.)

[Further readings: Isaiah 2; 11; 24; 49; 65.]

7) Heightened Levels of Global Bloodshed

The process of bringing forth justice to the nations is illustrated with vivid portrayals of bloodshed. These images are also consistent with John's descriptions found in Revelation.

> Who is this who comes from Edom,
> in crimsoned garments from Bozrah,
> he who is splendid in his apparel,
> marching in the greatness of his strength?
> "It is I, speaking in righteousness,
> mighty to save."
> Why is your apparel red,
> and your garments like his who treads in the winepress?
> "I have trodden the winepress alone,
> and from the peoples no one was with me;
> I trod them in my anger
> and trampled them in my wrath;
> their lifeblood spattered on my garments,
> and stained all my apparel." (Isa 63:1–3 ESV)

Incidentally, Edom is synonymous with red; it is believed that the Edomites had red hair (Genesis 25:30).

The account in Isaiah 34 also corroborates the level of bloodshed involved in the restoration of the earth. Isaiah tells us that the Lord has a sword that is dripping with blood.

> Their slain shall be cast out,
> and the stench of their corpses shall rise;
> the mountains shall flow with their blood ....
> The LORD has a sword; it is sated with blood;
> it is gorged with fat,
> with the blood of lambs and goats,
> with the fat of the kidneys of rams.
> For the LORD has a sacrifice in Bozrah,
> a great slaughter in the land of Edom. (Isa 34:3, 6 ESV)

[Further readings: Isaiah 34; 63.]

8) Global Celebration after Messiah's Triumph

After the cleansing of the earth, there will be a celebratory banquet with people of all nations, tribes, and tongues in attendance. This is in direct response to the salvation of the righteous and the extermination of the wicked.

> On this mountain the LORD Almighty
> will prepare a feast of rich food for all peoples,
> a banquet of aged wine—
> the best of meats and the finest of wines. (Isa 25:6 NIV)

The corresponding celebration in the Book of Revelation is known as the "marriage supper of the Lamb," where equivalently people of all nationalities come to celebrate their betrothal to Jesus, the bridegroom revealed.

Isaiah does not directly call it a wedding, but given that his writings on these events contain widespread use of bridal language, a connection between the two seems very plausible.

> As a young man marries a young woman,
> so will your Builder marry you;
> as a bridegroom rejoices over his bride,
> so will your God rejoice over you. (Isa 62:5 NIV)

> Sing, barren woman,
> you who never bore a child;
> burst into song, shout for joy,
> you who were never in labor ....
> For your Maker is your husband—
> the LORD Almighty is his name. (Isa 54:1, 5)

[Further readings: Isaiah 24–27; 62; 64–66.]

9) Supernatural Protection of the Righteous

In the midst of the ensuing carnage on the earth and its inhabitants, Isaiah makes sure to mention that the righteous servants will somehow be offered supernatural protection. Isaiah offers two explanations and also mentions that these righteous servants will experience heightened excitement and joy during this process. For instance, as mentioned previously, chapter 34 addresses this event from the perspective of the wicked while chapter 35 from the view of the righteous.

1) Hide yourself for a while

The first explanation occurs in Isaiah 26:20 where the righteous are instructed to hide in their rooms until the wrath (Isaiah 24–27) has passed. There are quite a few examples in the Old Testament of this sort of thing. For instance, Daniel and his friends are protected from fire, hungry lions, etc. We also have an account in the book of Revelation of a symbolic woman who is hidden in a desert and given supernatural care by the Lord himself. Isaiah doesn't offer many details on how it will occur specifically; nonetheless, the result and general idea is made clear.

> Go, my people, enter your rooms
> and shut the doors behind you;
> hide yourselves for a little while
> until his wrath has passed by.
> See, the LORD is coming out of his dwelling

to punish the people of the earth for their sins.
The earth will disclose the blood shed on it;
the earth will conceal its slain no longer. (Isa 26:20–21 NIV)

2) Good grapes

The second explanation, as you may recall from chapter 5, is illustrated through a familiar vineyard and grapes metaphor. "I will sing for the one I love a song about his vineyard" (Isa 5:1 NIV).

As before, the people of Israel are figuratively spoken of as a vineyard. Since they had become a rebellious nation, the prophetic message is that they would be destroyed since they did not produce the grapes the vinedresser was expecting.

By comparison, in the related illustration found in chapter 65, Isaiah also compares the nation of Israel to a cluster of grapes. However, this cluster within the vineyard is found to contain "juice" and, consequently, will be salvaged from the imminent destruction.

> As when juice is still found in a cluster of grapes
> and people say, "Don't destroy it,
> there is still a blessing in it,"
> so will I do in behalf of my servants;
> I will not destroy them all. (Isa 65:8 NIV)

Additional examples of this concept are found in Revelation, where in one instance God's servants metaphorically become a cluster of grapes, now "fully ripe" (Revelation 14:18).

Additionally, in another passage (following the sixth seal) John informs us that God's righteous servants will be protected. Before one of the angels releases this seal of judgment on the earth, he is halted and given the command to wait until these servants are identified and spared: "Do not harm the land or the sea or the trees until we put a seal on the foreheads of the servants of our God" (Revelation 7:3 NIV).

We are not told exactly how the cluster will be salvaged; nonetheless, the message is clear that God's righteous servants are not the target of God's wrath.

3. As in the days of Moses, the righteous will laugh, but the wicked will wail.

Isaiah makes it clear that the righteous will experience unparalleled joy and happiness during this execution of judgment on the earth.

> My servants will sing
> out of the joy of their hearts,
> but you will cry out
> from anguish of heart
> and wail in brokenness of spirit. (Isa 65:14)

He also compares these events to the days of Moses, as when the plagues were released in Egypt upon Pharaoh.

> Then his people recalled the days of old,
> the days of Moses and his people—
> where is he who brought them through the sea,
> with the shepherd of his flock? (Isa 63:11 NIV)

Thus, whether the righteous are hidden or protected, we do not know. Nonetheless, joy will be their main sentiment.

Other biblical passages (such as in Psalm 149) support the same idea, even suggesting that the elation experienced by the righteous servants (saints) is due to their participation in executing judgment on wickedness (see v. 9 below).

> May the praise of God be in their mouths
> and a double-edged sword in their hands,
> to inflict vengeance on the nations
> and punishment on the peoples,
> to bind their kings with fetters,
> their nobles with shackles of iron,

to carry out the sentence written against them—
this is the glory of all his faithful people. (Psalm 149:6–9 NIV)

A plethora of other passages throughout the scriptures can shed light on this scenario; the reader is encouraged to study other eschatological texts while taking into account the explanations that Isaiah has mentioned here.

[Further readings: Isaiah 26:20; 63; 65:8.]

Conclusion: Isaiah's threepeat, more than just a charm.

As we have seen throughout the classification of prophecies into various time periods (Buckets A, B, and C), Isaiah's vision of world history is quite unusual. From his vantage point, in 700 BC, he was able to foresee the rise and fall of nations all the way through the early first century AD; he was able to describe events appearing to include critical details in the life of Jesus of Nazareth; furthermore, he provides a plethora of eschatological glimpses into the future reign of a Davidic king.

Every year during the collegiate basketball playoff season, known as March Madness, fans have the ability to fill out brackets predicting how they expect teams to perform. One Duke University mathematics professor, Dr. Jonathan Mattingly, has calculated the likelihood of a perfect bracket to be one in 2.4 trillion.[2] Yet, by way of analogy, Isaiah seems to know the fate of world powers and has produced a perfect bracket of Mesopotamian history centuries in advance.

How did Isaiah know the events of world history? How was he able to describe the events in the life of Jesus with such specificity? Given Isaiah's predictive success in accurately depicting events in Buckets A and B, how much more relevant should his predictions concerning the end of human history be to us now?

Below is a chart summarizing the predictions we have studied in this section.

	Caption	Date Fulfilled	Reference
Bucket A			
	Emmanuel, the decline of Syria, and the Lost Tribes	732 BC	7-8, 17:1-14, 28
	Failed Assyrian invasion not by human hands	701 BC	8, 31:8-9, 30:32, 37
	Demise of Assyria	612 BC	10, 14:24-27, 30
	The abandonment of Tyre	607 BC	23:1,15, Ezekiel 26
	Rise of Babylon	605 BC	13-14, 21:9, 39, 43:14, 48:14
	Babylonian Captivity	597 BC	39, 5:13
	Defeat of Babylon	539 BC	13, 20, 44
	Medo-Persian Alliance	549 BC	13:17-18, 21
	Cyrus the Great	538 BC	44, 45
	Heliopolis and 5 Hebrew cities in Egypt	300 BC	19:18
	Jewish worship in Egypt	150 BC	19:19
Bucket B			
	The Servant rejected by his own people	33 AD	53:6
	The Servant will not retaliate	33 AD	50:6, 53, Mk 15, Lk 23:9, Mt 26:67
	The Lord's Servant Murdered	33 AD	50,52,53
	The Servant recieves a proper burial, even with the rich	33 AD	53:9
	The Servant's atoning death for "My People"	33 AD	53
	The Servant comes back to life	33 AD	53:11
	The Lord's Servant venerated outside of Jewish nations	33 AD	42:1, 49
Bucket C			
	Multinational worship of the Jewish God in Mt. Zion	-	2, 24
	The Complete Destruction of the Babylonic Empire	-	13, 14, 47
	Natural Catastrophes and Widespread Bloodshed	-	34, 63
	Extermination of Wickedness	-	2, 11, 24, 49, 65
	Supernatural Protection of the Righteous	-	26:20, 63, 65:8
	Destruction of the Earth replaced by New Heavens and New Earth	-	13:13, 24, 66
	The establishment of World Peace	-	2, 9, 11, 65:25
	Celebration After Messiah's Triumph	-	24-27, 62, 64-66
	God's Anointed Messiah will govern perpetually	-	9

*References without a book title are found in Isaiah

Fig. 8.1: Summarizing Isaiah's Prophecies

PART 3

VISIONS OF DIVINE PERSONALITY

LOGICAL BLUNDERS

CHAPTER NINE

As was mentioned earlier, the Bible is best viewed not as a single book but rather as a collection of books, a library consisting of many diverse texts. The myriad of writers contributing to the canon of scriptures offer perspectives from a vast array of sociocultural backgrounds (kings, peasants, philosophers, unschooled fishermen, etc.), and therefore consideration of an author's background is of indispensable value when studying a book in the Bible.

In the case of Isaiah, a brief survey of his biography indicates that he was a member of the Jerusalem aristocracy and, consequently, was granted access to a proper education.[1] The variety of literary styles found in his volume (narrative, song, poetry, history, etc.) shows his breadth and exposure to culture and art.

As a tenant in the royal palace of Jerusalem, he served as an adviser to four kings. It is speculated that he was the first cousin of King Uzziah, perhaps explaining why he was so devastated by his sudden death in chapter 6.[2]

One would expect accuracy, coherence, and logical communication to be traits of one with such a background—the producer of a prophetic masterpiece like the book of Isaiah.

Yet, here we present the case that a careful reading of Isaiah will reveal several contradictions—stories, analogies, and metaphors that are not entirely consistent and even some blatant grammatical errors.

Let's begin by looking at some of these alleged inconsistencies and investigate what they have to say.

Botanically Challenged

Trees have always had significant symbolic meaning in various cultures, particularly in the Hebraic society of Isaiah's day, where even tribal and genealogical relationships were often expressed using arboreal verbiage.

In a predominantly agricultural society well acquainted with plants and trees, Isaiah makes widespread use of this language throughout his text. These are just some examples of the metaphors and images he uses: cucumber gardens, oak trees, terebinth trees, vineyards, the holy seed, the stump, the root, and the branch.

With this in mind, let's focus on one such usage found in chapter 11.

In this passage, we are (metaphorically) looking into the future as with a telescope, elevated by fantastic words of hope as he describes the coming messianic era accompanied by the restoration of ecology and the retribution of wickedness, among other things.

Utilizing the metaphor of "the branch" and "the stump of Jesse" (developed throughout these passages: Isaiah 4:2; 6:13; 11:1, 10; 53:2), Isaiah goes further this time, also documenting the genealogy of this messianic figure.

According to verse 1, this individual will be a descendant of David — coming from Jesse's family line: "There shall come forth a Rod from the stem of Jesse." The Hebrew word describing the relationship here is *netzer*, defined as a sprout, shoot, or branch. The word is often used in reference to one's descendents as in a family tree.[3]

Yet in the same passage, he claims that this same person will also come from the *roots of Jesse*. "And a Branch shall grow out of his roots" (Isaiah 11:1), thus indicating that this person is an ancestor of David.

Is he a descendant or an ancestor, Isaiah? Which one is it? One could be tempted to explain this away as an isolated event, a mere mistake in transcription, if not for its repeated usage in verse 10: the "Root of Jesse."

In that day there shall be a Root of Jesse,
Who shall stand as a banner to the people;
For the Gentiles shall seek Him,
And His resting place shall be glorious. (Isaiah 11:10)

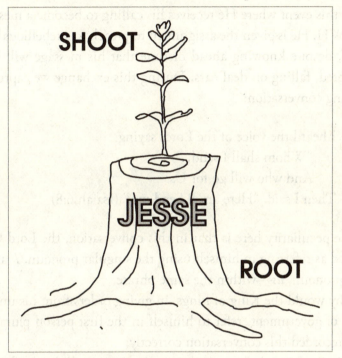

Fig. 9.1: *The Root and the Shoot of Jesse*

How can these two statements be reconciled?

Is this indeed a mistake or rather the communication of something more profound—a divine mystery concerning the identity of this figure? Is he implying that this messianic figure is timeless (existing both before and after David's lifetime), functioning as his ancestor *and* descendant?

In the last pages of the Bible, John hears Jesus making use of such phrases, applying both to himself: "I, Jesus, have sent my angel to testify to you about these things for the churches. I am the root and the descendant of David, the bright morning star" (Revelation 22:16 ESV)

Let's keep this in mind as we consider the remainder of these inconsistencies.

Grammarian's Nightmare

Another subtle inconsistency is found in chapter 6. In what is one of the most vivid displays of the majesty of God ever recorded in the books of the Bible, Isaiah has a direct encounter with almighty God. It is during this event where He receives his calling to become a messenger of YHWH. He is given the assignment to preach to a rebellious nation (Israel), despite knowing ahead of time that his message will largely be ignored, falling on deaf ears. During this exchange we capture the following conversation:

> I heard the voice of the Lord, saying:
> "Whom shall I send,
> And who will go for Us?"
> Then I said, "Here am I! Send me." (Isaiah 6:8)

The peculiarity here is that in this conversation, the Lord God is recorded as referring to himself using the singular pronoun, *I*, and the plural pronoun, *us*—within the same phrase.

Why would the King of kings, in giving orders from his universal throne of government, refer to himself in the first person plural? Has Isaiah recorded this conversation correctly?

A similar "mistake" occurs three other times in the book of Genesis; one of which is during the creation of Man, where the creative entity also refers to himself in the plural as *us*.

> Elohim said, Let Us make man in Our tzelem, after Our demut: and let them have dominion over the fish of the sea, and over the fowl of the air, and over the cattle, and over all the earth, and over every creeping thing that creepeth upon ha'aretz (the earth). So Elohim created humankind in His own tzelem, in the tzelem Elohim (image of Elohim). (Bereshis [Genesis] 1:26–27 OJB)

(See also Genesis 3:22 and Genesis 11:7 for additional examples.)

Hebrew language experts are said to agree that this passage employs an unusual use of grammar.[4]

In the original Hebrew Bible, the words *Adonai* and *Elohim* are used as reverent alternatives to YHWH and are found in both singular and plural forms (the latter being the most common). An example of this is in the opening line of Genesis: "In the beginning God created the heavens and the earth" (Genesis 1:1). Nonetheless, the pronouns attached to these titles are always used in the singular form throughout the Bible, apart from the cases we have mentioned above.

This inconsistency is somewhat bizarre, more so in the example found in Isaiah, since both forms are used in the same sentence.

Are these indeed "mistakes," or are they indicative of a deeper reality concerning God's nature?

ESCHATOLOGICAL MIX-UPS

CHAPTER TEN

In this section we traverse a brief survey of the deeds, actions, and attributes associated with several characters involved in Isaiah's vision of the future. The claim is that outlining a consistent description of these pivotal eschatological events becomes a daunting challenge due to a "disorganization" on Isaiah's part. Primarily, his predictions on key events such as: the establishment of *World Peace*, global adjudication through a *Supreme Judge*, and the universal execution of penalties via an *Executive Branch*. Let's investigate this dilemma further.

Agents of World Peace

One of the most prominent predictions in Isaiah's accounts of future days is the establishment of world peace—as seen in the grand account of Isaiah 2.

> He shall judge between the nations,
> and shall decide disputes for many peoples;
> and they shall beat their swords into plowshares,
> and their spears into pruning hooks;
> nation shall not lift up sword against nation,
> neither shall they learn war anymore. (Isa 2:4 ESV)

What a glorious day!—when nations will not learn war anymore, when instruments hitherto used for destruction and mass killings will instead be used for agriculture and building society. In verse 3, Isaiah informs us that the agent to perform these actions will be the God of Jacob, "Elohim Yacob"—one of the revered titles for Almighty God. Surely, only he could carry out such an enormous feat.

Yet by the time we reach chapter 9, we are immersed in another very similar account of world peace. This time, however, the agency responsible for its fruition is not the God of Jacob but a "Son" yet to be born. The similarity between these two accounts indicates that they are both referring to the same event.

Isaiah's account states that military personnel and the armed forces will lead the charge in burning their instruments of warfare, as their utility in this newfound utopia has been diminished to simply "fuel for the fire."

> For every boot of the tramping warrior in battle tumult
> and every garment rolled in blood
> will be burned as fuel for the fire. (Isa 9:5 ESV)

To the careful reader the question naturally arises, who is the agent of world peace, Isaiah? Is it the "God of Jacob" or the "Son to be born"?

In his description, he goes on further to reveal the identity of this son. We learn that he is in possession of some unique titles: Prince of Peace, Everlasting Father, Wonderful, Counselor. What kind of child is this who will bring about world peace, even possessing characteristics of immortality, ruling perpetually from David's throne?

Perhaps examining another subsequent account of future days found in chapter 11 will help clarify the situation. Can we identify a party responsible for such a monumental accomplishment?

> The wolf will live with the lamb,
> the leopard will lie down with the goat,
> the calf and the lion and the yearling together;
> and a little child will lead them.
> The cow will feed with the bear,
> their young will lie down together,

and the lion will eat straw like the ox.
The infant will play near the cobra's den,
and the young child will put its hand into the viper's nest.
They will neither harm nor destroy
on all my holy mountain. (Isa 11:6–9)

In this beautiful account of global restoration, peace extends beyond just harmonious relations with humans and spreads into the animal kingdom.

Nonetheless, we are left no closer to determining the agency of world peace after examining this account, as it is attributed to "the Root" and "the Shoot"—a mysterious individual who, as we saw previously, is both an ancestor and a descendant of David.

As if matters have not been sufficiently obfuscated by this point, another description in chapter 65 also fails to clarify the dilemma.

Here, the Lord Adonai makes a series of declarations detailing actions that *he* will perform in the face of Judgment; one of which is copied almost verbatim from chapter 11 and previously applied to "The Root" and "The Shoot."

> "Behold, it is written before Me:
> I will not keep silence, but will repay—
> Even repay into their bosom ….
> The wolf and the lamb shall feed together,
> The lion shall eat straw like the ox,
> And dust shall be the serpent's food.
> They shall not hurt nor destroy in all My holy mountain,"
> Says the LORD. (Isa 65:6, 25)

Again, the similarity in phrasing gives the impression that this is referring to the same event.

So who will be the agent of world peace, Isaiah? Is it the God of Jacob, a Son to be born, the Prince of Peace, the Shoot, the Root from Jesse, the Lord Adonai? According to these passages we have just examined, the best answer would have to be "all of the above." Let's examine the remaining attributes to determine if we can shed some light on this dilemma.

Judicial Branch

Mankind has always dreamed of a global utopia: a world where all nations coexist peacefully, where bloodshed and warfare are relics of the past. One of the greatest challenges to this end is arriving at a balanced notion of justice—a universal consensus on what fairness looks like to all parties. In such a scenario, who would have the authority to arbitrate the affairs of humanity? Who has the objective perspective into global affairs, the capability to decide on matters with complete equity and impartiality?

Here in Isaiah's vision of future days, we catch a glimpse of one who steps in to make such judgments at a global level; a supreme "Judicial Branch" whose justice is flawless. As with before, let's try and establish the identity of this individual.

Throughout the scriptures, the Lord God is frequently given the title as supreme *Judge*: "The Lord is our judge, the Lord is our lawgiver, the Lord is our king; it is he who will save us" (Isaiah 33:22 NIV).

This is echoed again in Isaiah 2, where the "God of Jacob" is claimed to be the one who will judge between nations and settle disputes. Nonetheless, despite Isaiah's clearly singling out the Lord God as the Supreme Judge of the universe, some of these personalities which we have previously mentioned are also attributed with administering absolute justice. "The Child to be born" from chapter 9 will be seated on David's throne and execute justice, as well as "the Root" and "the Shoot" who, according to Isaiah, will also judge the earth and provide justice for the needy.

> With righteousness he will judge the needy,
> with justice he will give decisions for the poor of the earth.
> He will strike the earth with the rod of his mouth;
> with the breath of his lips he will slay the wicked. (Isa 11:4)

Additionally, not only will these familiar characters sit in the position as "Supreme Judge," but the Servant from the second half of Isaiah will also perform the same task. It is somewhat curious as to how this servant will bring forth justice, considering that Isaiah predicts he will not open his mouth.

> Behold! My Servant whom I uphold,
> My Elect One in whom My soul delights!
> I have put My Spirit upon Him;
> He will bring forth justice to the Gentiles. (Isa 42:1)

Again we are puzzled with the question: how many Supreme Judges are there? Is it the God of Jacob, the Child, the Root, the Branch, or the Servant of the Lord? Once again, the best answer, after studying these passages, is "all of them."

Executive Branch

Love is a violent flame. One of the most often misunderstood aspects of God's character is the relentless pursuit of his bride throughout time. His promise of eternal covenant with Israel—the descendants of Abraham, Isaac, and Jacob—is interpreted by many as one of the greatest examples of true love and marriage.

When taken out of context, however, the bloodshed and warfare involved in that pursuit can seem rather unwarranted. How can a God of love sanction acts of war and judgment? Yet in the midst of this imminent carnage and widespread destruction, we learn of history's most epic battle taking place at the end of the age. It is a campaign rooted in the beauty of a romanced bridegroom longing to be reunited with his bride; a removal of everything that hinders love.

Herein we unfold Isaiah's good news of hope: justice will not only be proclaimed one day but executed publicly. As mentioned previously, the arrival of this savior-bridegroom on the scene will serve to identify two groups. The first will experience joy, interpreting these events as a reason for grand celebration; the second will experience fear and trembling as they are confronted head-on by the jealous bridegroom.

Let us try to understand who this individual is.

From Isaiah 2, we first observe how the God of Jacob takes the seat of the Executive Branch.

In what resembles the chorus from a song, notice the similarities in phrasing of the following three passages:

> Enter into the rock, and hide in the dust,
> From the terror of the LORD
> And the glory of His majesty. (Isa 2:10)
>
> They shall go into the holes of the rocks,
> And into the caves of the earth,
> From the terror of the LORD
> And the glory of His majesty,
> When He arises to shake the earth mightily. (Isa 2:19)
>
> To go into the clefts of the rocks,
> And into the crags of the rugged rocks,
> From the terror of the LORD
> And the glory of His majesty,
> When He arises to shake the earth mightily. (Isa 2:21)

Continuing our examination, we return to chapter 11, where "the Root" and "the Shoot" also seem to share this responsibility, as they will strike the earth with words of their mouth.

> With righteousness He shall judge the poor,
> And decide with equity for the meek of the earth;
> He shall strike the earth with the rod of His mouth,
> And with the breath of His lips He shall slay the wicked.
> (Isa 11:4)

Similarly, this same act of inflicting terror on the wicked is also mentioned in chapter 65. Here, however, the Lord God (Adonai) is the responsible party.

> You shall leave your name as a curse to My chosen;
> For the Lord G<small>OD</small> will slay you,
> And call His servants by another name. (Isa 65:15)

The question arises once again, who will strike the earth with terror in bringing forth justice? The God of Jacob, the Root, the Shoot, or the Lord Adonai? Once again, the answer given by the text is "all of the above."

Oneness rant

So far, we have seen how multiple personalities perform similar actions and share seats with the God of Jacob. One possible explanation for Isaiah's apparent madness is that perhaps he was a polytheist. Could these personalities simply be other gods aiding the God of Jacob in his responsibilities?

This position, however, is difficult to maintain in light of Isaiah's emphatic mentions of the oneness of the Jewish deity. In fact, perhaps no other prophet throughout the scriptures presents a stronger case for monotheism and the oneness of God than does Isaiah.

This is seen through a series of rhetorical questions and titles appearing in chapters 41–55, in the following forms: "Who Is my equal?" "To whom will you compare me? says the Holy One"; etc. (Isaiah 40:25; 43:10; 44:8; 45:5; 45:14; 45:21).

These titles are sprinkled around through this section, bolstering successive defenses to the supremacy of the Jewish deity. They almost form a list of accolades describing just how high and lofty he is in comparison to every other entity in existence.

In light of these passages, the polytheistic hypothesis becomes difficult to sustain. How then can these seemingly conflicting claims be reconciled?

So far, we have considered Isaiah's description of "the Root" and "the Shoot," who is both a descendant and an ancestor of David; the grammatical errors in referring to God with plural and singular pronouns; and finally the various personalities claiming their identity as Supreme Judges, Executors, and Agents of World Peace.

In formulating a hypothesis, the reader is encouraged to consider what other biblical writers have documented on the topic of divine personhood. The answer that emerges is quite elegant and—though paradoxical at face value—not foreign to our human experience.

For the student of physics, this paradox is quite familiar, as seen in our current understanding of the nature of light. Let's take a quick detour to investigate.

Wave–Particle Duality

In 1704, Isaac Newton published his seminal work defending his view of the "particle theory of light" in *Opticks*.[1] As a highly venerated scientist, his publication convinced many that at the most fundamental level, light was a particle. His demonstrations provided evidence showing that just like everyday material objects, light exhibited characteristics such as reflection, refraction, and the ability to travel through a vacuum without a medium.

Despite the successes of the particle theory of light, a Dutch mathematician, Christian Huygens, readily disagreed with Newton's conclusions, instead introducing the "wave theory of light."[2] In his treatise, he began by demonstrating that Newton's observations on reflection would also be true if light was a wave. Then he exposed critical deficiencies in Newton's particle theory by showing that when light refracts through a medium (such as water), it actually behaves like a wave. Newton remained mostly silent with regard to Huygens's findings.

The wave theory of light remained unchallenged for some time until scientists like Max Planck and Einstein (through discoveries in quantum mechanics), showed that light behaves like a particle as well![3]

Thus, science's best answer to the question, "Is light a particle?" is a resounding "Yes!". At the same time, science's best answer to the question, "Is light a wave?" is also "Yes!". This phenomenon is known as the wave–particle duality of light.

Is it surprising—if, according to natural science, light exists in multiple natures—that such a posited supernatural entity as the "Light of the World" would do so as well? The testimony of divine persona in the Isaiah scroll readily attests to this paradox.

NEW TESTAMENT ALLUSIONS

CHAPTER ELEVEN

Given the rarity of our encounters with phenomena like wave–particle duality in everyday life, it seems fitting to briefly explore what other books of the Bible might have to say about this topic in our efforts to arrive at a more comprehensive conclusion. Does their testimony corroborate the description of God presented by Isaiah, or is he alone in this estimation?

We will begin by examining how other biblical writers have interpreted and applied Isaiah's writings. The claim here is that the characteristics attributed to the *one* monotheistic Jewish deity (found in Isaiah) have been taken and applied to another individual—namely, Jesus of Nazareth.

Honors

Every knee will bow

In Isaiah's emphatic address on the uniqueness of the Jewish deity (chapters 41-55), we learn of a very distinct honor conferred to God, particularly, that all of humanity will one day bow prostrate and verbally acknowledge Him as supreme. As is typical in this section, the statement is prefaced with the customary redundant chants, "There is no other God besides me", "I am God and there is no other", etc., further emphasizing his singularity and authority as God.

> I have sworn by Myself;
> The word has gone out of My mouth in righteousness,
> And shall not return,
> That to Me every knee shall bow,
> Every tongue shall take an oath. (Isa 45:23)

With the context of this passage in mind, let's consider another well-known passage in the New Testament where Paul (in his letter to the Philippians) references the same distinct honor, this time, however, ascribing it to the person of Jesus.

> At the name of Jesus every knee should bow, of those in heaven, and of those on earth, and of those under the earth, and that every tongue should confess that Jesus Christ is Lord, to the glory of God the Father. (Philippians 2:10–11)

As a well studied Pharisee—said to have exceeded his peers in Judaism—Paul's familiarity with the writings of Isaiah can be presumed.[1] This is evidenced not only in the borrowing of this title, but curiously he also mentions the "Servant of the Lord" at the beginning of this address in verse 7 (a phrase which Isaiah uses extensively in this section). Thus, Paul seems to have been intentional with his choice of words, essentially applying to Jesus Christ a title thus far reserved for YHWH.

His usage of this phrase is not limited to this address to the Philippians but also appears in his letter to the Romans:

> It is written:
> "As I live, says the LORD,
> Every knee shall bow to Me,
> And every tongue shall confess to God." (Romans 14:11)

Has Paul just committed the same logical error that we have seen throughout Isaiah? First (in Philippians), the title is borrowed from Isaiah and applied to Jesus; but then in the second occurrence (Romans), he applies the same passage to YHWH. What is Paul implying here?

By representing these aforementioned claims as a syllogism, we would have the following argument. If both premises are true, then the conclusion follows naturally.

Syllogism:

1. YHWH is the only one to which every knee will bow and tongue confess (Isaiah 45:23).
2. At the name of JESUS every knee will bow and tongue confess (Philippians 2:10–11).
3. JESUS is YHWH.

Thus, if we introduce this seemingly paradoxical hypothesis, namely, that Jesus is YHWH, the alleged contradictions by the various writers instead become accurate depictions of divine personhood. As was the case with the wave–particle duality of light, it would be foolhardy to dismiss this hypothesis simply on the basis of its paradoxical nature.

Titles

The First and the Last

Similarly, in another portion of Isaiah's oneness rant on the uniqueness of God, YHWH is assigned the title of "the First and the Last."

This distinctive of God expresses that he alone is ageless, even existing outside of space and time. Every other god (or idol) simply fails this test, and Isaiah insists that only YHWH could ever meet this criterion.

> Thus says the LORD, the King of Israel,
> And his Redeemer, the LORD of hosts:
> "I am the First and I am the Last;

Besides Me there is no God." (Isa 44:6 NKJV)

It should be pointed out that the title is used several times throughout the book, also occurring at Isaiah 41:4 and 48:12.

With this knowledge in mind the student of the book of Revelation will notice John making widespread use of this title. Sometimes he is explicit in utilizing the exact phrasing, "the First and the Last"; other times he uses slightly different words to express this notion of timelessness, such as in "the alpha and omega," "the beginning and the end," or even in the phrase "the one who was, is, and is to come."

Each time, however, they are applied to Jesus Christ who, according to John, holds this title. As the author of the book entitled *The Unveiling* or *The Revelation of Jesus Christ*, what is the view of Jesus he is trying to communicate here?

> saying, "I am the Alpha and the Omega, the First and the Last," and, "What you see, write in a book and send it to the seven churches which are in Asia: to Ephesus, to Smyrna, to Pergamos, to Thyatira, to Sardis, to Philadelphia, and to Laodicea." (Revelation 1:11)

Other uses of this title can be referenced in the following passages: Revelation 1:8, 18; 21:6; 22:13.

From studying these two books, the evidence leads us to affirm that both YHWH and Jesus share the title of being "the First and the Last." So which one is it? Yes!

Characters

Bridegroom/Husband

We continue exploring the attributes Isaiah assigned to the divine that are applied to Jesus in the New Testament by considering the personality of the "bridegroom" or "husband."

Throughout the Old and New Testaments, the theme of the

bridegroom is quite prominent. For instance, many times throughout the Old Testament, the nation of Israel is portrayed as a wife who has been unfaithful to her husband, YHWH. The story of Hosea and Gomer is a representation of this relationship; Hosea, a righteous man, is asked to marry a prostitute named Gomer.

The theme is also present throughout Isaiah's volume. For instance, following the story of the Suffering Servant and his gruesome death in chapter 53, Israel is personified as a "barren woman." Isaiah predicts that this woman will have a plethora of children and should therefore respond with rejoicing and song: "Sing, Barren Woman," "Enlarge your tents," etc. The principal reason is that YHWH will become her husband, and her offspring will be more than those of a married woman.

> Your Maker is your husband,
> The LORD of hosts is His name;
> And your Redeemer is the Holy One of Israel;
> He is called the God of the whole earth. (Isa 54:5)

Similarly, in chapter 62, Isaiah depicts Israel as being the wife of YHWH. Though she has been trampled upon, He will not remain silent in defending Israel. The bridal language used in this chapter illustrates this point effectively; Israel will be a royal diadem in the hand of God, her land will be married and YHWH himself is to be the husband of Israel.

> As a young man marries a virgin,
> So shall your sons marry you;
> And as the bridegroom rejoices over the bride,
> So shall your God rejoice over you. (Isa 62:5)

The bridal theme of God and Israel continues throughout a plethora of books and passages in the New Testament. In contrast, most of the occurrences here attribute this character to the person of Jesus Christ.

The incidences are so many and varied that we will illustrate with only a couple.

Why don't your disciples fast?

In one incident, Jesus is questioned about fasting. The Pharisees have difficulty understanding why John's disciples fast but the disciples of Jesus do not. He replies with the following words:

> Jesus said to them, "Can the friends of the bridegroom fast while the bridegroom is with them? As long as they have the bridegroom with them they cannot fast. But the days will come when the bridegroom will be taken away from them, and then they will fast in those days." (Mark 2:19–20)

Thus, in identifying himself as the "Bridegroom," Jesus states that once he is no longer with them, they can resume the practice of fasting.

In the Gospel of John, John the Baptist also affirms Jesus as the "Bridegroom," considering himself to be simply a "friend of the Bridegroom." When his life's call and statements are taken into account, it becomes apparent that his function was to point to Jesus.

> You yourselves bear me witness, that I said, "I am not the Christ," but, "I have been sent before Him." He who has the bride is the bridegroom; but the friend of the bridegroom, who stands and hears him, rejoices greatly because of the bridegroom's voice. Therefore this joy of mine is fulfilled. (John 3:28–29)

Similar identifications of Jesus as the Bridegroom are made by Paul, where he understands his mission to present the Church to Jesus as a chaste virgin.

> I am jealous for you with a godly jealousy. I promised
> you to one husband, to Christ, so that I might present
> you as a pure virgin to him. (2 Corinthians 11:2 NIV)

Furthermore, one could hardly miss this case in the last scene of Revelation where John is shown the actual wedding ceremony of the Lamb: the Church being prepared as a bride for Jesus.

The reader is encouraged to consider the following passages, where, repeatedly, the Old Testament metaphor of the "Husband of Israel" is applied to Jesus: Ephesians 5:23; Revelation 19; 21:2, 9.

Though these predictions seem a bit difficult to visualize—that the creative deity of the universe could somehow enter into marriage with a people group— as we have seen, throughout the scriptures (Old and New Testament), Jesus is *also* a party to God's eternal (marriage) covenant with the descendants of Abraham, Isaac, and Jacob. This leads us to the conclusion that both YHWH and Jesus are acting as the personality of the "Bridegroom."

Savior

Another title that both YHWH and Jesus share is that of Savior.

> Truly You are God, who hide Yourself,
> O God of Israel, the Savior! (Isa 45:15)

> I, even I, am the Lord,
> And besides Me there is no savior. (Isa 43:11)

These declarations are both times prefaced with Isaiah mentioning that there is no other God besides him. Once again, we are in the middle of the oneness rant, and the case for the distinctiveness of the Jewish deity is supported all the more with the inclusion of this title: "He alone is savior."

Examining the New Testament writings, we find the same title applied various times to the person of Jesus Christ. Consider the following two examples:

> Looking for the blessed hope and glorious appearing of our great God and Savior Jesus Christ. (Titus 2:13)

> Simon Peter, a bondservant and apostle of Jesus Christ,
> To those who have obtained like precious faith with us by the righteousness of our God and Savior Jesus Christ. (2 Peter 1:1)

What is interesting about these examples is that not only do the writers attribute the title of "Savior" to Jesus but, according to Sharp's rule for interpreting New Testament Greek, both nouns, *God* and *Savior*, apply to the one person, Jesus Christ, and therefore explicitly attribute the title of God to Jesus as well.[2]

Actions

Next, in this section, we examine various actions that both the Old Testament deity and Jesus seem to perform.

Creation of the Cosmos

The first of these acts is that of being responsible for creation. As we have seen previously (during Isaiah's oneness rant), he is very explicit about YHWH's *sole* involvement in the creation of the world, even taking great lengths in mentioning that these acts were performed "by myself" or with "my own hands."

Additional examples of these statements can be found in these passages: Isaiah 37:16; 40:12; 42:5; 44:24; 45:12; 48:13; 51:13.

Below is one such example:

> This is what the LORD says—
> your Redeemer, who formed you in the womb:

> I am the LORD,
> the Maker of all things,
> who stretches out the heavens,
> who spreads out the earth *by myself.* (Isa 44:24 NIV, italics added)

> It is I who made the earth
> and created mankind on it.
> *My own hands* stretched out the heavens;
> I marshaled their starry hosts. (Isa 45:12 NIV, italics added)

In surveying the New Testament in the attempt to answer the question, "Who is responsible for creation?", our claim is that this responsibility attributed to YHWH is also shared with Jesus. Below are some examples of this attribution:

> All things were made through Him, and without Him nothing was made that was made …. He was in the world, and the world was made through Him, and the world did not know Him. (John 1:3, 10)

> By him all things were created, in heaven and on earth, visible and invisible, whether thrones or dominions or rulers or authorities—all things were *created through him* and for him. (Colossians 1:16 ESV, italics added)

> In these last days he has spoken to us by his Son, whom he appointed the heir of all things, through whom also *he created the world.* (Hebrews 1:2 ESV, italics added)

The New Testament writers—mostly coming from a Jewish background—were undoubtedly very aware of the monotheistic tradition in Judaism; that only God (YHWH) is responsible for this creative work.³ What are the implications of giving Jesus such creative powers?

Supreme Executive Branch Revealed

Finally, recalling the *Eschatological Mix-Ups* we studied earlier, where according to Isaiah multiple personalities (the Root, the Shoot, the Branch, etc.) are performing the same actions at the end of the age, we will extend this analysis to the New Testament, where Jesus finds himself among the characters in this mix-up.

Specifically, consider the passage we saw previously in Isaiah 2, where in an almost chorus-like fashion it is repeated that the wicked will "hide in caves from the terror of the Lord" (see Isaiah 2:10, 19, 21).

In the book of Revelation, we again come across these words, but now they are being applied to Jesus Christ.

> Then the kings of the earth and the great ones and the generals and the rich and the powerful, and everyone, slave and free, hid themselves in the caves and among the rocks of the mountains, calling to the mountains and rocks, "Fall on us and *hide us* from the face of him who is seated on the throne, and from the wrath of the Lamb, for the great day of their wrath has come, and who can stand?" (Revelation 6:15–17 ESV, italics added)

The similarities of these accounts in Isaiah and Revelation suggest that they are referring to the same event. Thus, we ask John and Isaiah, "Who will these unrighteous leaders hide from during the terror of this Judgment?" Isaiah says the God of Jacob; John says Jesus Christ. Who is correct?

Below is a diagram with scripture references summarizing some of the relationships we have explored thus far:

	YHWH	The Child	The Shoot	The Root	Suffering Servant	Y'shua (Jesus)
World Peace	[2:4,65:25]	[9:5]	[11:9]	[11:9]		Lk 2:14
Judicial Branch	[2:4,33:22]	[9:7]	[11:3,4]	[11:3,4]	[42:1]	Rev. 19:11
Executive Branch	[2:10,19,21] [65:6,15]	Ps. 2:9	[11:4]	[11:4]		Rev. 6:15, 19:15
Every Knee Will Bow	[45:23], Rm. 14:11					Phil. 2:10
Bridegroom (Husband)	[54:5, 62:5]					Mk. 2:19, Jn. 3:29 Rev. 19, 21:2,9
Savior	[45:15,33:22]					2 Pt. 1:1, Ti. 2:13
King	[33:22]	[9:6,7], Ps. 2:6		Rm. 15:12		Rev. 19:16, 11:5
Creation	[37:16, 40:12, 44:24, 42:5, 45:12, 48:13, 51:13]					Jn. 1:3,10, Col. 1:16, Heb. 1:2
Gentiles Seek	[2:2]			Rm. 15:12, [11:10]	[42:4, 49:6]	Rm. 9:24
First and the Last (Timeless)	[44:6, 41:4, 48:12]	[9:6]				Rev. 1:8,11,18, Rev. 21:6, 22:13
YHWH		[9:6]				
The Root				[11:1]		
Y'shua (Jesus)			Rev. 22:16			

*References to the Book of Isaiah are included within brackets (e.g. [1:1] = Isaiah 1:1)

Fig. 11.1: *Summary of Divine Attributes and Personalities in Isaiah*

Occam's Razor and Hypostatic Union

As we bring our thoughts to a close, the aim is that the presentation of these apparent inconsistencies will motivate readers to further search the scriptures in formulating their own personal views on the identity of the person of Christ.

Our own position is that the conclusion, "Jesus is YHWH," is not only the simplest explanation but also the most elegant, for it ties the Servant of the Lord to the King of kings. This conclusion, though inherently paradoxical, is one of the most beautiful messages of the Christian faith, that a being so high and exalted would become the servant of all; he wears a crown and washes feet. The man of many sorrows is set to be the earth's greatest political leader.

According to Isaiah, we have yet to witness the greatest love pursuit of all. His affections are expressed not only in the historical records—which document his covenant relationship with Israel—but will also be displayed through the power of his coming, ultimately leading in a grand wedding celebration. We consider his name, *Y'shua* (God saves), which incidentally is Isaiah's name reversed, *Yeshayahu* (salvation comes from God).

Throughout the scriptures we are told that only God is worthy of worship. The angel in Revelation 22:9 did not allow himself to be worshipped. Yet by way of contrast, from the woman caught in adultery to the wise men arriving from across the globe through celestial signs, Y'shua receives their worship.

May he forever receive ours.

A QUESTION OF AUTHORSHIP:
DID MORE THAN ONE PERSON WRITE ISAIAH?

APPENDIX

The predictive content in Isaiah would seem less than impressive if it could be demonstrated (convincingly) that Isaiah is not the sole author of his volume, that the book was rigged and these predictions were added after the fact by other authors.

Many have contemplated this possibility. The first documented dissent on the single authorship of Isaiah occurred in 1129 by Moses Ben Samuel.[1] His position resurfaced with greater influence in the eighteenth century through the efforts of theologians like Bernhard Duhm, Koppe, and other Enlightenment thinkers.[2]

Today modern biblical scholars remain divided on the issue, with a majority holding the view that at least more than one person is responsible for Isaiah.[3] Among these scholars, further discourse exists on exactly how many writers were involved and where these divisions should occur. Below are the most prominent divisions:

"First" or "Proto" Isaiah supposedly wrote chapters 1–39.

"Second" or "Deutero" Isaiah supposedly wrote chapters 40–55.

"Third" or "Trito" Isaiah supposedly wrote chapter 56–66.

What reasons are there for adopting these divisions? What advantage, if any, will adopting this view hold? Furthermore, are there any underlying philosophical assumptions that seem to be made in presenting this case?

Cyrus is Mentioned by Name

The most common argument for postulating multiple authors is a claim that certain sections were written at different times during the Babylonian Exile because of the information they contain with regard to certain events, particularly that of naming the famed Medo-Persian leader, Cyrus the Great (Isaiah 44:28–45:1).

How could an eighth-century writer know the name of a world leader almost 200 years before his appearance? Surely, the section containing this prediction must have been written by someone after Cyrus's rise to power at the end of the Babylonian Exile.

Proto "First" Isaiah made predictions that were fulfilled after his lifetime

At first glance, this hypothesis seems like a more reasonable explanation of the Cyrus prophecy. However, it does not completely dissolve the special revelation dilemma it attempts to solve.

That is, if we have but one instance of a prediction from "Proto" Isaiah being fulfilled during the Babylonian Exile, the strength of this argument is severely diminished.

As we have presented in Part 2, *Isaiah's Panoramic Perspectives*, Isaiah 1–39, the section that critics attribute to "Proto" Isaiah, contains such predictions. Among them are the rise and fall of both Assyria and Babylon, the establishment of the Medo-Persian alliance, and the prosperity of the Jews in Egypt occurring some 466 years after the writing. (Consult *Isaiah's Panoramic Perspectives* for a fuller list of their fulfillments.)

In light of Isaiah's panoramic perspective, foreknowledge of the rising world leader, Cyrus, is hardly a challenge. Assuming multiple authors on the basis of this foreknowledge adds no strength to an argument.

Style and Fragmentation: Moot

Another commonly cited reason for multiple authorship is an alleged disunity of the book in terms of style and geographical setting. More specifically, the claim is that the writings in the separate halves do not reflect the work of the same author and that the metaphors in the second half are Babylonian and not Palestinian. However, upon a careful examination of the phraseology in the text, this claim is simply not true.

Elements of Style

Let's explore the first question. What evidence would we expect to find in supporting the multiple authors hypothesis? Proponents of this view have alluded to a discontinuity in language, that the use of grammar and style suddenly changes. This position, however, appears to lose credence in light of a rather apparent observation, namely that there are multiple unique Isaianic phrases and images in both halves of the book, phrases which we seldom find in other biblical writings.

Below is a brief sample of such phrases:

"Holy One of Israel"

Perhaps the most apparent Isaianic phrase found in both halves is the expression "Holy One of Israel," appearing twelve times in chapters 1–39 and fourteen times in chapters 40–66. By way of comparison, it appears only five times in the rest of scripture.

First-half example: "In that day people will look to their Maker and turn their eyes to the Holy One of Israel" (Isa 17:7 NIV).

Second-half example: "Your Maker is your husband— the Lord Almighty is his name— the Holy One of Israel is your Redeemer; he is called the God of all the earth" (Isa 54:5 NIV).

"Wolf and Lamb"

Another example of a phrase used in both halves occurs in Isaiah 11 and 65. In both of these instances, the description of global restoration mentions the same image and metaphor.

> "The wolf and the lamb will feed together,
> and the lion will eat straw like the ox,
> and dust will be the serpent's food.
> They will neither harm nor destroy
> on all my holy mountain,"
> says the LORD. (Isa 65 NIV)

> The wolf will live with the lamb,
> the leopard will lie down with the goat, ...
> and the lion will eat straw like the ox ....
> They will neither harm nor destroy
> on all my holy mountain,
> for the earth will be filled with the knowledge of the
> LORD
> as the waters cover the sea. (Isa 11:6–9)

According to some scholars, there are more than forty sentences or phrases of this type that appear in both portions which are found in no other Old Testament book.[4]

Below are some of these examples illustrating similar uses of language in both halves:

First Half (Ch. 1-39)	Second Half (Ch. 40-66)
Isa 1:15 — Yes, even though you multiply prayers, I will not listen. Your hands are covered with blood.	Isa 59:3 — For your hands are defiled with blood And your fingers with iniquity;
Isa 11:9 — They will not hurt or destroy in all My holy mountain	Isa 65:25 — They will do no evil or harm in all My holy mountain
Isa 14:27 — "For the LORD of hosts has planned, and who can frustrate [it?] And as for His stretched-out hand, who can turn it back?"	Isa 43:13 — "Even from eternity I am He, And there is none who can deliver out of My hand; I act and who can reverse it?"
Isa 28:5 — In that day the LORD of hosts will become a beautiful crown And a glorious diadem to the remnant of His people;	Isa 62:3 — You will also be a crown of beauty in the hand of the LORD, And a royal diadem in the hand of your God.
Isa 35:6 — For waters will break forth in the wilderness And streams in the Arabah.	Isa 41:18 — I will open rivers on the bare heights And springs in the midst of the valleys; I will make the wilderness a pool of water And the dry land fountains of water.
Isa 35:10 — And the ransomed of the LORD will return And come with joyful shouting to Zion, With everlasting joy upon their heads. They will find gladness and joy, And sorrow and sighing will flee away.	Isa 51:11 — So the ransomed of the LORD will return And come with joyful shouting to Zion, And everlasting joy [will be] on their heads. They will obtain gladness and joy, And sorrow and sighing will flee away.

*References from NASB

Fig. A.1: Similar Uses of Language in Both Halves of Isaiah

Given the abundance of these phrases, the statement that there is a disparity of language in both halves is simply not true.

Some critics have responded by saying that the latter writers of Isaiah borrowed these phrases and images in an attempt to sound "Isaianic," at which point the discussion becomes circular, and any conclusions drawn from language considerations become irrelevant.

Babylonian Metaphors in the Second Half

The same type of breakdown occurs when considering another similar but slightly more specific claim; namely that there is an abrupt change of scenery in the second half, evidenced by the choice of descriptive words. According to this hypothesis, the second half, written in Babylon, contains metaphors, images, and other phrases resembling Babylon rather than Palestine.

This claim is also not true. This fact has been pointed out by many biblical commentators who observe Isaiah's mention of features such as the taxonomy of trees, bodies of water, and geological features mentioned in both halves that are native to Palestine. Furthermore, they note the absence of typical Babylonian geological features.[5]

Here is a brief sample of such geographical features in the text:

"Cut Down Cedars"

> By your messengers you have ridiculed the Lord.
> And you have said,
> "With my many chariots
> I have ascended the heights of the mountains,
> the utmost heights of Lebanon.
> I have cut down its tallest cedars,
> the choicest of its junipers.
> I have reached its remotest heights,
> the finest of its forests. (Isa 37:24 NIV)

> He cut down cedars,
> or perhaps took a cypress or oak.
> He let it grow among the trees of the forest,
> or planted a pine, and the rain made it grow. (Isa 44:14 NIV)

Other instances of Palestinian trees discovered by the *Pulpit Commentary* in both halves are: oaks, firs, pines, box trees, sycamores, cypresses, shittah trees, olives, vines, and myrtles. They have also observed that the palm tree, which is native to Babylon, is not mentioned.

Continuing further, an examination of the bodies of water in Isaiah also suggests a Palestinian setting. For instance, the streams, brooks, fountains, pools (reservoirs), and springs mentioned (Isaiah 15:7; 22:11; 30:25; 35:7; 41:18; 48:21; 58:11, etc.) are Palestinian. Furthermore, the absence of the Euphrates River (the life and sustenance of Babylon) illustrates that this claim is extremely weak.

While, as we have mentioned previously, there is a clear shift in perspective at chapter 40, there is not (as the divisionists have suggested) a fundamentally foreign style to the rest of the text.

As we identified in Part 1, *Homologously Encrypted*, Isaiah's book contains about ten sections. Utilizing the same reasoning, should we then suspect the existence of ten different authors?

As a collection of several types of writings, does it make more sense that Isaiah wrote differently about different topics at different points of his life rather than speculating about multiple authors?

Considering Isaiah's background as a member of the royal family, this is not difficult to imagine. Nonetheless, the onus of proof lies with the critic to show that a shift in perspective in his collection must somehow *only* imply a different author.[6]

Further Complications

At this point, not only does the multiple authors hypothesis seem to offer no added explanatory power, but if accepted, it presents greater challenges than it attempts to solve.

Who are the other authors of Isaiah?

One of the challenges the multiple authors hypothesis faces is in identifying the authors for second or even third Isaiah.

Observe below a typical opening found in Hebrew Old Testament prophetic books.

> The vision concerning Judah and Jerusalem that Isaiah son of Amoz saw during the reigns of Uzziah, Jotham, Ahaz and Hezekiah, kings of Judah. (Isa 1:1 NIV)

> The words of Jeremiah son of Hilkiah, one of the priests at Anathoth in the territory of Benjamin. (Jeremiah 1:1 NIV)

> The vision of Obadiah. This is what the Sovereign LORD says about Edom. (Obadiah 1:1 NIV)

The opening line in Isaiah's prophecy follows this typical template and clearly attributes the entire work to Isaiah. If according to critics additional contributors were involved, where is the address to "Deutero" or "Trito" Isaiah?

Lesser known prophets (such as Obadiah, Nahum, Haggai, etc.), even from the same Babylonian era, were remembered, yet somehow we are expected to overlook the fact that one of Israel's greatest writers, "Deutero-Isaiah" (chapters 40–55), has been forgotten. Moreover, the divisionists must also explain why these works were combined with Isaiah's if they were written at a much later date—an explanation conspicuous by its absence throughout the centuries.

Early Historians

Another challenge faced in adopting a multiple authors position is the record of history. The earliest ancient documents in our possession affirm that Isaiah is the sole author of the book.

For instance, in the apocryphal Book of Sirach, circa 200 BC, we find references to both halves of Isaiah as being attributed to the same individual.

> In Isaiah's time, the sun moved backward,
> and he extended the king's life.
> By his great spirit,
> he saw what was to come,
> and he comforted those
> who mourned in Zion. (Sirach 48:23–24 CEB)

The historian Josephus also believed Isaiah to be the sole author of the book, even citing that Cyrus read Isaiah's prophecy in reference to himself.[7]

Furthermore, as Theologian Edward J. Young points out, in the following passages the New Testament frequently quotes from Isaiah and affirms Isaiah as the sole author:[8]

Matthew 3:3; 8:17; 12:17; 13:14; 15:7; Mark 7:6; Luke 3:4; 4:17; John 1 :23; Acts 8:28, 30, 32, 33; 28:25; Romans 9:27, 29; 10:16, 20.

No archeological evidence

Another challenge for divisionists is the lack of archaeological evidence demonstrating that Isaiah was ever split up or considered separate entities. Rather, the earliest manuscripts of Isaiah promote the idea that the writings were intended to be one unit.

For instance, the scrolls from Q1 in Qumran, circa 300 BC, have placed Isaiah 40 right after chapter 39 with no indication of a split. This is particularly curious as chapter 39 was found toward the end of the scroll; it would have been convenient to begin on the next column of parchment, yet this was not the case.[9] No ancient evidence exists for splitting them up.

Underlying Assumption of Naturalism

As we summarize the evidence concerning the authorship of Isaiah, it is important, as in any other objective inquiry, that the evidence itself should lead us to the best explanation.

New discoveries are typically made when we are forced to open up within our own premises in light of the evidence.

Here, it appears that divisionists have been motivated by the underlying assumption of naturalism and the desire to avoid explanations that invoke special revelation and divine insight into human affairs. As we have demonstrated, resorting to a divisionist view of Isaiah does not avoid implications toward this position and further, in light of the surrounding evidence, only raises more questions than it answers. The possibility of supernatural revelation must at least be considered by the critic, an idea alluded to in chapters 40–44, where Isaiah makes the claim that supernatural knowledge (and revelation to his servants) is the hallmark of YHWH's authenticity and what separates him from the other (false) gods and useless idols.

REFERENCES

Introduction

1. Brooke, G., 1997. *Writing and Reading the Scroll of Isaiah, Volume 2*. Brill, 609–632. See Also Dss.collections.imj.org.il. 2020. *The Digital Dead Sea Scrolls*. [online] Available at: <http://dss.collections.imj.org.il/isaiah> [Accessed 10 March 2020].
2. Kaminsky, J., and A. Stewart, 2006. God of All the World: Universalism and Developing Monotheism in Isaiah 40–66. *Harvard Theological Review*, 99(02).
3. Jull, A., D. Donahue, M. Broshi, and E. Tov, 1995. Radiocarbon Dating of Scrolls and Linen Fragments from the Judean Desert. *Radiocarbon*, 37(1): 11–19.
4. Dss.collections.imj.org.il. 2020. *The Digital Dead Sea Scrolls - Isaiah*. [online] Available at: <http://dss.collections.imj.org.il/isaiah> [Accessed 24 March 2020].

Chapter 1: Mile-High Synopsis

1. Raghav, 2009. *Motivating Thoughts of Stephen Hawkings*. Prabhat Prakashan, 40.
2. Arntzenius, Frank, and Tim Maudlin, 2002. Time Travel and Modern Physics" *Royal Institute of Philosophy Supplement* 50: 169–200. doi:10.1017/S1358246100010560.
3. Birnbaum, S., 1951. Notes on the Internal and Archaeological Evidence concerning the Cave Scrolls. *Journal of Biblical Literature*, 70(3): 227–232.
4. Moore, G. F., 1893. The Vulgate Chapters and Numbered Verses in the Hebrew Bible. *Journal of Biblical Literature* 12(1): 73–78. Accessed March 10, 2020. doi:10.2307/3259119.
5. Negev, A. and S. Gibson, 2005. *Edom; Edomites. Archaeological Encyclopedia Of The Holy Land*. New York. Continuum, 149–150.

Chapter 2: Structural Similarities

1. Moore, G. F., 1893. The Vulgate Chapters and Numbered Verses in the Hebrew Bible. *Journal of Biblical Literature* 12(1): 73–78. Accessed March 10, 2020. doi:10.2307/3259119.
2. Josephus, F., and H. Thackeray, 2004. *The Life; Against Apion*. Cambridge, Mass.: Harvard University Press, Book 1 #8.
3. Jewish Publication Society of America, 1917. *The Holy Scriptures According to the Masoretic Text*. Philadelphia.
4. Graetz, Heinrich, 1871. Der alttestamentliche Kanon und sein Abschluss (The Old Testament Canon and its finalisation). *Kohélet, oder der Salomonische Prediger (Kohélet, or Ecclesiastes)* (in German). Leipzig: Carl Winters Universitätsbuchhandlung, 147–173.
5. Bruce, F., 1988. *The Canon of Scripture*. IVP Academic, 215. See also Gamble, H., 2002. *The New Testament Canon*. Philadelphia: Wipf & Stock, 271.
6. Eusebius of Caesarea, *Ecclesiastical History* Book v. Chapter v. See also Tertullian, *Adversus Marcion*, 4.2 See also Ntcanon.org., 2010. *The Development of the Canon of the New Testament - Authorities*. [online] Available at: <http://www.ntcanon.org/authorities.shtml> [Accessed 11 March 2020].
7. Irenaeus, *Against Heresies*. Book III 11.8.
8. Jacobsen, A., 2009. *The Discursive Fight over Religious Texts In Antiquity*. Aarhus: Aarhus University Press, 168. See also original text Athanasius, *39th Festal Letter in the year 367*.
9. Irenaeus, *Against Heresies*. Book III 11.9.
10. Irenaeus, *Against Heresies*. Book I 31.1.
11. Kruger, M., 2012. *Canon Revisited: Establishing the Origins and Authority of the New Testament Books*. 1st ed. Crossway.
12. Pawson, David, 2010. *Come with Me through Isaiah*. Oxford eBooks Ltd., ch 1. See also Liebreich, Leon J., 1956. The Compilation of the Book of Isaiah. *The Jewish Quarterly Review* 46(3): 259–277.

Chapter 3: Old Testament Parallels

1. Pawson, David, 2012. *Unlocking the Bible*. HarperCollins UK, ch 21: Isaiah.
2. Stone, Tim, 2010. Review of Steinberg, Julius, Die Ketuvim: ihr Aufbau und ihre Botschaft (BBB, 152; Hamburg: Philo, 2006). *The Journal of Hebrew Scriptures* 10. See Also Koorevaar, Hendrik J., 2010. The Torah model as original macrostructure of the Hebrew canon: A critical evaluation. *Zeitschrift für die alttestamentliche Wissenschaft* 122(1): 64–80.

Chapter 4: New Testament Parallels

1. Rawlinson, Henry Creswicke, and John Gardner Wilkinson, 1861. *The history of Herodotus*. vol. 1.
2. Mallowan, Max, 1972. Cyrus the Great (558–529 BC). *Iran* 10(1): 1–17. Josephus, F., n.d. *The Antiquities of the Jews*. General Books, Book 11, Chapter 1.
3. Pawson, David, 2012. *Unlocking the Bible*. HarperCollins UK, ch. 39, Luke and Acts. See also Mauck, John W., 2001 *Paul on Trial: The Book of Acts as a Defense of Christianity*. T. Nelson Publishers.
4. Bauckham, Richard, 1996. Josephus Account of the Temple in Contra Apionem 2.102–109." In *Josephus' Contra Apionem*, Brill, 327–347. See Also Deut. 23.

Chapter 5: Bucket A: Historical Predictions

1. Torrey, Chas., 1928. *C. The Second Isaiah*. New York: Charles Scribner's Sons.
2. Knibb, Michael A., 1985. Martyrdom and Ascension of Isaiah. *The Old Testament Pseudepigrapha* 2: 143–176. See also Gray, George Buchanan, 1912. *A critical and exegetical commentary on the Book of Isaiah*, Vol. 1. Clark, 72
3. See Strong's H5959. "Hebrew Dictionary (Lexicon-Concordance)." Study Bible Key Words in Hebrew/Aramaic & Greek with Strong's Numbers. Accessed March 16, 2020. http://lexiconcordance.com/hebrew/5959.html. See also Miller, Clyde M., 1979. Maidenhood and Virginity in Ancient Israel. *Restoration Quarterly* 22: 242–246.
4. Dubovský, Peter, 2006. Tiglath-pileser III's campaigns in 734-732 BC: Historical background of Isa 7; 2 Kgs 15-16 and 2 Chr 27-28." *Biblica*: 153–170. See also Nadali, Davide, 2009. "Sieges and Similes of Sieges in the Royal Annals: The Conquest of Damascus by Tiglath-Pileser III." *Kaskal* 6: 137–149.
5. Bacon, Ewa K., 2010. The Dynamics of Ancient Empires: State Power from Assyria to Byzantium. *Journal of World History* 21(4): 734–738. See also Anirudh. "Anirudh." Learnodo Newtonic, September 12, 2018. https://learnodo-newtonic.com/assyrian-empire-facts.
6. Cogan, Mordechai, 2001. Sennacherib's siege of Jerusalem: Once or twice? *Biblical Archaeology Review* 27(1): 40.
7. Oded, Bustenay, 1998. History vis-à-vis Propaganda in the Assyrian Royal Inscriptions. *Vetus Testamentum*: 423–425.
8. McNeill, William H., n.d. Infectious Alternatives: The Plague That Saved Jerusalem, 701 BC. *What if?: The World's Foremost Military Historians imagine What Might Have Been*.
9. Goodspeed, George Stephen, 1913. *A History of the Babylonians and Assyrians*. London: Smith, Elder, ch. 9, 270.

10　Frahm, Eckart, 2017.The decisive blow came in 612, when Babylonian and Median armies, after a two-month long siege, conquered Nineveh. *A Companion to Assyria.* Hoboken: John Wiley & Sons.

11　Wiseman, D. J., 1956. *Chronicles of Chaldaean Kings: (626-556 BC) in the British Museum.* London: Trustees of the British Museum, 99.

12　Bradley, Patrick J., and Deborah Levine Gera, 1996. Xenophon's 'Cyropaedia.' *The Classical World* 89(6): 88–89.

13　Clayton, Peter A., and Martin Price. *The seven wonders of the ancient world.* Routledge, 2013, 38.

14　Álvarez-Mon, Javier, and Mark B. Garrison, eds., 2011. *Elam and Persia.* Winona Lake, IN: Eisenbrauns, 91.

15　Potts, D. T., 2003. *Mesopotamian Civilization: the Material Foundations.* London: Athlone, 22–23.

16　Josephus, Flavius, 1900. *The antiquities of the Jews.* Routledge, bk. 11, ch. 1.

17　Hanson, Ann Ellis, and Aryeh Kasher, 1987. The Jews in Hellenistic and Roman Egypt: The Struggle for Equal Rights. *The American Historical Review* 92(2): 392. See also Safrai, S., and M. Stern, 1974. The organization of the Jewish communities in the Diaspora. In *The Jewish People in the First Century,* vol. 1. Brill, 464–465.

18　Bohak, Gideon, 1995. Joseph and Aseneth and the Jewish temple in Heliopolis. 3878–3878. See also Last, Richard, 2010. "Onias IV and the δέσποτος ερός: Placing Antiquities 13.62–73 into the Context of Ptolemaic Land Tenure." *Journal for the Study of Judaism* 41(4–5): 494–516. See also Mason, Steve, 2008. *Flavius Josephus: Translation and Commentary, Volume 1b: Judean War 2.* Brill, vii. 10, #3.

19　Wallace, S., 2018. Alexander the Great and Democracy in the Hellenistic World. In *The Hellenistic Reception of Classical Athenian Politics and Political Thought*, Oxford University Press, 45–72.

20　Poole, Reginal Stuart, 1882. *The Cities of Egypt, by Reginald Stuart Poole.* London: Smith, Elder and Co., ch. 8.

21　Mahaffy, Sir John Pentland, 1899. *A History of Egypt under the Ptolemaic Dynasty.* London: Methuen & C., 192.

22　Joosten, Jan, 2012. *Collected Studies on the Septuagint: From Language to Interpretation and Beyond.* Tübingen: Mohr Siebeck, 185–239. See also Dines, Jennifer M., and Michael Anthony Knibb, 2005. *The Septuagint.* London: T & T Clark.

23　Egypt Exploration Society, 1888. *Memoir of the Egypt Exploration Society.* Vol. 2. Trübner, 18-19.

24　Josephus, Flavius, 1900. *The antiquities of the Jews.* Routledge, 13.2, 13.69.

25　Kratz, Reinhard G., 2006. "The Second Temple of Jeb and of Jerusalem." *Judah and the Judeans in the Persian Period*: 247. See also Sacchi, Paolo, 2004. *The History of the Second Temple Period.* London: T. & T. Clark, 151.

Chapter 6: Identifying the Lord's Servant

1. Westermann, Claus, 2000. *Isaiah 40–66: a Commentary*. Philadelphia: Westminster Press, 92.
2. Orlinsky, Harry Meyer, and Norman Henry Snaith, 1967. *Studies on the Second Part of the Book of Isaiah*. Vol. 14. Brill Archive, 12. See also Duhm, Bernhard, 1892. *Das Buch Jesaia*. Göttingen: Vandenhoeck & Ruprecht.
3. "A symbolic name for Israel as supremely happy or prosperous" <Entry for: Jeshurun> Peloubet, F. N., M. A. T. Peloubet, and William Smith, 2014. *Smith's Bible Dictionary*. Peabody, MA: Hendrickson.
4. Malul, Meir, 1996. 'āqēb "Heel" and 'āqab "To Supplant" and the Concept of Succession in the Jacob–Esau Narratives. *Vetus Testamentum*: 190–212.
5. Hirsch, S., I. Levy, and M. Hirsch, 2005. *Hirsch Commentary on the Torah*. Brooklyn, N.Y.: Judaica Press, Genesis 33:4. See also Hacohen, Malachi Haim, 2019. *Jacob & Esau: Jewish European History between Nation and Empire*. Cambridge University Press, 238.

Chapter 7: Bucket B: Messianic Predictions

1. Bockmuehl, Markus N. A., and Christopher M. Tuckett, 2012. *The Cambridge Companion to Jesus*. Cambridge: Cambridge University Press, 123–124.
2. Hengel, Martin, 1989. *Crucifixion in the Ancient World and the Folly of the Message of the Cross*. Philadelphia: Fortress Press.
3. Bauckham, Richard, 1996. Josephus Account of the Temple in Contra Apionem 2.102–109. In *Josephus' Contra Apionem*, Brill, 327–347.
4. Feldman, Bronson. "Barabbas and the Gospel of Yeshua the Galilean." *American Imago* 39, no. 3 (1982): 181-93. Accessed July 28, 2020.
5. Lyons, William, 2004. On the life and death of Joseph of Arimathea. *Journal for the Study of the Historical Jesus* 2(1): 29–53.
6. Wright, Nicholas Thomas, 2003. *The Resurrection of the Son of God*. Vol. 3. Fortress Press.

Chapter 8: Bucket C: Eschatological Predictions

1. UN.org, 2020. *Charter Of United Nations Chapter I*. [online] Available at: <https://www.un.org/en/sections/un-charter/chapter-i/index.html> [Accessed 14 March 2020].
2. 2. Math.duke.edu, 2020. *Duke Math Professor Says Odds Of A Perfect Bracket Are One In 2.4 Trillion | Department Of Mathematics*. [online] Available at: <https://math.duke.edu/news/duke-math-professor-says-odds-perfect-bracket-are-one-24-trillion> [Accessed 14 March 2020].

Chapter 9: Logical Blunders

1   Porton, G., 1976. *Isaiah and the Kings: The Rabbis on the Prophet Isaiah.* Leiden: E.J. Brill, 694.
2   Bible.ucg.org, 2020. *Introduction to Isaiah.* [online] Available at: <http://bible.ucg.org/bible-commentary/Isaiah/Sins-of-Israel-and-Judah-like-scarlet/> [Accessed 14 March 2020].
3   Biblehub.com, 2020. *Strong's Hebrew: 5342.* נֵצֶר *(Netser) -- A Sprout, Shoot.* [online] Available at: <https://biblehub.com/hebrew/5342.htm> [Accessed 14 March 2020].
4   Walsh, J., 2017. *Style and Structure In Biblical Hebrew Narrative.* Collegeville, MN: Liturgical Press, 105. See also Hasel, G., 1975. *The Meaning of "Let Us" in Gn 1:26.* Berrien Springs: Andrews University.

Chapter 10: Eschatological Mix-Ups

1   Newton, I., 1704. *Opticks: Or, A Treatise of the Reflexions, Refractions, Inflexions and Colours of Light.*
2   Huygens, Christiaan, and Silvanus P. Thompson, 2010. *Treatise on Light.* Memphis, TN: General Books, ch. 1.
3   Greiner, Walter, and Berndt Müller, 2001. *Quantum Mechanics: with 88 Worked Examples and Problems.* Berlin: Springer.

Chapter 11: New Testament Allusions

1   Young, Brad H., 1995. *Paul the Jewish Theologian: A Pharisee among Christians, Jews, and Gentiles.* Baker Books.
2   Sharp, Granville, 1803. *Remarks on the uses of the definitive article in the Greek text of the New Testament; containing many new proofs of the divinity of Christ, from passages which are wrongly translated in the common English version. To which is added an appendix containing i. A table of evidences of Christ's divinity, by dr. Whitby. ii. A plain argument from the gospel history for the divinity of Christ, by the editor [T. Burgess]. To which is added two other appendices,* 8.
3   Calvert-Koyzis, Nancy, 2004. *Paul, monotheism and the people of God: the significance of Abraham traditions for early Judaism and Christianity.* Vol. 273. Bloomsbury Publishing.

Appendix: A Question of Authorship: Did More Than One Person Write Isaiah?

1. George A. Buttrick et al., eds., 1956, *The Interpreter's Bible,* vol. 5. New York: Abingdon Press, 382.
2. Young, E., 1984. *An Introduction to the Old Testament.* Wm. B. Eerdmans Publishing, 204.
3. Stromberg, Jacob, 2011. *An Introduction to the Study of Isaiah.* Bloomsbury Publishing, 2.
4. Archer, Gleason, 1998. *A Survey of the Old Testament Introduction:* 3rd ed. Chicago: Moody Press. 382.
5. Spence, H. D. M., and Joseph S. Exell, eds., n.d. *The Pulpit Commentary: Isaiah,* vol. 1. New York: Funk & Wagnalls Company.
6. Margalioth, Rachel, 1964. *The indivisible Isaiah: evidence for the single authorship of the prophetic book.* Sura Institute for Research.
7. Josephus, Flavius, 1900. *The antiquities of the Jews.* Routledge, 11.12.
8. Young, Edward J., 1967. The Authorship of Isaiah. *Themelios* 4: 11–16.
9. Flint, Peter W., 2012. The Interpretation of Scriptural Isaiah in the Qumran Scrolls: Quotations, Citations, Allusions, and the Form of the Scriptural Source Text. In *A Teacher for All Generations* Vol. 1. Brill, 389–406.